SECRETS TO INNER BEAUTY

VISION HOUSE PUBLISHERS
Santa Ana, California 92705

Secrets to Inner Beauty

Copyright © 1977 by Vision House Publishers, Santa Ana, California 92705.

Library of Congress Catalog Card Number 77-87103
ISBN 0-88449-071-8

Printed in the United States of America.

CONTENTS

To my wife Ruthe, who has been a continual source of inspiration and joy to me, and taught me much about beauty.

To Stephen and Kristen, our children, who are a constant delight and challenge.

Words of Gratitude:

"As iron sharpeneth iron, so a man sharpeneth the countenance of his friends." God has used many people to mold my life to this point. I wish to express my appreciation to four such men in particular. To my father, whose consistent and godly life set a great example to me. To "Uncle John" (Dr. John G. Mitchell), whose faithful preaching of the word and radiant love for Christ helped me see Christ in His beauty. To "Pete" (Peter Scruggs), my fourth grade Sunday School teacher whose example of faithfulness and service marked me for life. To "Prof" (Dr. Howard Hendricks), who loved me and believed in me at a crucial point in my life.

I am also extremely grateful to the board of elders at Mariners Church whose love for me and for each other has been a thing of beauty.

I am indebted to Nayda Wallace, Lawana Norman and Patty Baker for their faithfulness in typing and editing the manuscripts, and for their ideas and suggestions which helped shape this work.

FOREWORD

Many of us are wearing our years to shreds without any awareness that God has planned for us a life that is always fresh, forever fulfilling, and intrinsically beautiful. Discovering that life is what this book is all about.

"The first qualification for judging any piece of workmanship from a corkscrew to a cathedral," said C. S. Lewis in his introduction to *Paradise Lost*, "is to know *what* it is—what it was intended to do and how it is meant to be used." Dr. Aldrich is here looking at life to find its loveliness and perceptively examines the working parts: marriage, parenting, everyday doings.

He has an eye for *good* workmanship. I have loved and appreciated Joe as a student, as my teaching assistant, and as a beloved brother and colleague in the gospel ministry. He has always been a keen observer.

Some years ago I purchased what I believed to be a new car at a bargain price. Joe wanted to give it a basic wax and polish job. As we stood back to admire the sparkling finish under the bright Texas sunshine, Joe pointedly asked: "Prof, are you aware that this car has been repainted? And look at this . . . it's been damaged . . ."

Sure enough, the imperfections were evident when they were pointed out. Joe is that kind of scout.

Like the coverup paint job, ugliness, deceit and sham too often hide the beauty in our lives. "God is beauty," Joe states. "As partakers of His nature we can be beautiful." He explores the road to beauty by moving to matters of the heart; he speaks of conscience and lifestyle. Beauty becomes an attainable ideal, not the impossible dream, as Dr. Aldrich reveals the One who is the Way, the Truth, and the Life, the Creator of beauty, the Architect of symmetry in life.

May I suggest you dive in; it's a literary beauty bath!

—Howard G. Hendricks

INTRODUCTION

I took my boy to see Santa Claus, and underneath the paint and pillows was a dirty old man. Visions of sugar plums danced across the stages of our minds until the camera broke and the cash flow stopped. Saint Nick lost his cool, and the spirit of Christmas was dealt a mortal blow. Santa got caught with his sales slip showing. He tarnished his sainthood. What I experienced was ugly. Not wicked, not unusual, but ugly. Ugly because Santa's actions as a person contradicted my idealized expectations. Mr. X under the paint and pillows was hired to be beautiful, to be consistent with our culture's carefully prescribed role for him. We expect Santa to have unity and completeness, the integrity of the whole. Dear old St. Nick proved to be ugly because there was an evident lack of balance. Even though his concern for the broken camera was legitimate, we were disappointed that his desire for gain outshadowed his consideration of his helpers.

What then should we do? Shatter the myth of an always kind, benevolent granddaddy who never sweats, frowns or swears? Should we let him float from chimney to chimney as a greater-than-life man or cut him down to size?

For the idealized world of children, we'd best leave Santa alone, and hope his slip doesn't show too often. But for us grown-up folks, perhaps we can learn a lesson from Santa's paint and pillows. Let's take inventory for a moment. When we were children, we believed in Santa. But then we came of age and with a sense of mistiness proclaimed "there is no such thing as Santa Claus." So far, so good. Now the bad news. Look closely at your wardrobe and mine. Black boots and belt, white beard, red hat with a tassel, pillow (for some) and a big bag full of goodies. We believed in him, we denied him, and then we embraced his life-style and became little Santas.

You say, "I'm not a Santa Claus, I'm a predispensational millennialist." That's good. But you're also a sinner. Sin inclines us to be Santa Clauses—people who put on costumes to hide our liabilities and change our identities. Adam was the first one to run for the paint and pillows. He wore fig leaves. Sin made him a fugitive, and his children have been hiding ever since. Satan had told him he would "be like God." Man has been trying to "be like God" ever since, and in the process has gone a long way toward destroying his true humanity. He cannot cope with his wickedness and as a result neglects his wonder. The great race today is not for the moon, it's for the paint and pillows.

What a Santa Sinner Looks Like

Perhaps we can gain some insight by reflecting on what a Santa sinner looks like. 1) Usually he wears a false face. The rouge, wig and false whiskers pretty well hide the real thing. It's important that his "slip" does not show. He keeps up a good front, surrounded as he is by worshipping children, Mrs. Claus and all his sweet little helpers. An ill wind seldom blows at the North Pole. At least the weatherman never reports it.

2) He always smiles and says "Ho Ho Ho!" a lot. The children may pull his whiskers, life's flashbulbs may blind his eyes and aggravate his headache, but he bites a bullet and continues to "grin and bear it." The pasted-on smile and stained-glass voice pretty well conceal his status anxieties and bleeding ulcers. "Things are always great at the North Pole, Ho Ho Ho." His motto is "the right face in the right place."

3) He always has a bag full of goodies. Why else is he revered? These are bartered away for affection, attention and the right to remain "anonymous" behind the paint and pillows. "A toy a day keeps reality away." It takes a lot of time, sweat and energy to keep the bag full of goodies and so Santas feel excused from "everyday trivia" because of their noble calling. Santas have been known to weep when the goodies run out, but such "weakness" is usually well concealed.

4) He flies in the fog. When visibility is zero, he follows the glowing nose of Rudolf, the ugly duckling deer. Santas wouldn't think of having a co-pilot along. Alone with his reindeer and bag full of goodies, he flies off into the fog with what appears to be reckless abandon, and usually is.

5) He always gets through despite insurmountable obstacles. We don't know of a single failure. If Mrs. Claus does, she's silent about it. Failure makes Santas ugly. They try fairly hard to cover it, and usually succeed.

The Pharisees were masters of the paint and pillow. Remember the Pharisee (see Luke 18:9-14) who thanked God he was "the real thing" and condemned the poor sinner? Jesus said he was flying in the fog, totally out of touch with reality. He was ugly when compared with reality. Jesus said the Pharisees were like burial vaults, all gussied up on the outside, but full of ugliness and corruption on the inside. Yet, the Pharisees said many right things, and

9

preached much that was true. They had a lot of goodies in their bags. They believed in God, they believed the Scriptures were divine and authoritative, and they believed in the resurrection of the dead. The Pharisees condemned adultery, cheating, lying and stealing. They were very concerned that the law of God be central in their thoughts and actions. In spite of all the "goodies" they did not have the approval of God. They handled, discussed and debated truth, and yet their lives produced ugliness. Somehow their daily diet of doctrine didn't seem to result in love, joy, peace and longsuffering. In spite of their glorious claims, Christ called them hypocrites. Hypocrisy is ugly.

The Goal Is Love

Most of us aren't members of the sect of the Pharisees. Perhaps the church of Ephesus is a better model for us. In his letter to his friends at Ephesus, Paul used Christ's love to illustrate the great truth that *love's purpose is to call forth beauty*. Christ's love takes a blemished bride (the church) and makes her beautiful, not having ugly stains, blemishes or wrinkles (5:25-27). He loves the church so that He can "present her to himself as a radiant church," (5:27, NIV). Love calls forth beauty from ugliness.

Paul reminded Timothy, the pastor at Ephesus, that love was the goal of all his instruction and teaching. "The goal [ultimate end] of our instruction is love . . ." (I Tim. 1:5, NASB). Notice what he didn't say. He didn't say that the "goal of our instruction is to make everyone Calvinists," or "the goal of our instruction . . . the whole aim and purpose of our ministry . . . is to make everyone premillennial dispensationalists, or to fill their frontal lobes with facts." No, he tells his friend that the ultimate test of his ministry is whether or not the truth he communicates develops men and women characterized by a lifestyle of love. We will take a good look at love in a later chapter. At this point it is significant to note that the quality of love is the ultimate goal of all our efforts in ministry. Love is the distinctive brand of true Christianity . . . Christianity which produces beauty.

In Ephesians 1:15 Paul commends his friends for their faith and love. Their belief in the living Christ and His radical life-style expressed itself in the way that they lived life together. Their faith worked itself out through love. It incarnated itself and became evident and visible as these dear brothers gave of themselves and their resources to care for one another.

John gives us another verbal snapshot of the church at Ephesus and enables us to see what happened to the church in the years following Paul's death. In the second chapter of Revelation, John records Jesus' evaluation of the church. He has a lot of good things to say about them. He commends them for their hard work and perseverance (see Rev. 2:2). They were not lazy and did not give up when the storm clouds gathered. They had a high level of commitment and dedication.

He commends them for their doctrinal purity. They would not tolerate wicked men who attempted to deceive the flock with false teaching. Certainly that was good. The Lord highlights their willingness to endure hardships for His sake. Their faith was costly, yet they didn't go into spiritual bankruptcy. Imagine being part of a church like this . . . hardworking, committed, doctrinally pure, willing to sacrifice anything and everything for the cause of Christ. This must have been an extraordinary church.

Yet our Lord is not content with what He sees. "Yet I hold this against you: You have forsaken your first love" (Rev. 2:4, NIV). It doesn't say they *lost* it. They had *replaced* it with something else. This was no small deviation or incidental flaw. "Remember the height from which you have fallen! Repent and do the things you did at first"

11

(Rev. 2:5, NIV). They abandoned their love for the Saviour in the busyness of learning and defending the faith. They got so involved in the details of the printer's ink, that they lost the Prince of Peace. The literal word swallowed up the living Word.

When a church forsakes its love for the Saviour, the wrinkles and blemishes start showing themselves again. The beauty and radiance which a love for the Saviour produces, fades rapidly when we focus on anything but Christ. The sad fact is that many churches and individuals end up holding tightly to the "truth," and yet produce ugliness. Love is one of God's divine footprints. Its presence spreads the fragrance of Christ everywhere. "All men will know that you are my disciples if you love one another" (John 13:35, NIV). Its absence presents the world with paint and pillows—a caricature of Christ and Christianity.

The Pharisees were certainly the "Super Santas" of their day. They were disgruntled with Christ because He didn't go along with the "games Pharisees play." His disciples gave them fits because they refused to be boxed in by the external trivia of a Pharisaical lifestyle. They ate with dirty hands, picked and ate grain on the Sabbath, and didn't fast at the right time. The Pharisees, suffering from "hardening of the categories," came to Jesus as "defenders of the faith" demanding to know why Christ allowed His followers to live such unruly lives. "Men of the cloth" were expected to live a cut above the commoners. Stained glass voices, folded hands, proper decorum, and an air of disdain were the distinguishing marks of the "holy" man. The Pharisees wanted Christ to launder His lifestyle, bleaching out any evidence of His association with "publicans and sinners." In their estimation, Christ and His disciples needed to go to finishing school to learn how to walk, talk and put on the paint and pillows. Christ's response to their charges deserves our careful attention. It may help us begin to let go of the security of the paint and pillows and reach out for the new wineskins.

New Wineskins Needed

In a nutshell, Christ told the Santas of His day that He was introducing a lifestyle so unique and radical it couldn't be bottled, sold and franchised. In Mark 2, He responds to their charges by describing a way of life so full of vitality and beauty that it cannot be sewn to the old garments, the pillows of religious externalism, or poured into and contained by the old wineskins. By nature, it seems, we are keepers of the old wineskins. The whole purpose of Paul's letter to the church at Galatia was to pull them away from the old wineskins, and get them to stand fast in the new liberty which Christ has provided for them.

The church at Ephesus gradually retreated to the old wineskins of a cold, ugly orthodoxy. They became God's frozen people. The Lord said their retreat was a great fall, a serious, grievous deviation. He followed his diagnosis with a warning: "If you do not repent, I will come to you and remove your lampstand from its place" (Rev. 2:5, NIV). When the people of Israel lost their love for Jehovah, and fell into religious externalism, God sovereignly removed His glory from the temple. It continued to function, sacrifices were still offered, rituals were still performed, yet the presence of God was not here.

Christ told the Church at Ephesus to let go of the old wineskins, to regain their love for the Saviour, or He would sovereignly remove the lampstand, the source of light and beauty. He doesn't say the church would not continue, that the services would end. The beauty of His presence would simply no longer grace their fellowship. The glory of God would depart. Paint and pillows . . . or the glory of God.

13

To turn from love of Christ and one another to anything else is a serious deviation. When love is lost, God would rather the church go out of existence than continue to hang on to old wineskins and perpetuate ugliness in the name of truth. Light can be hidden, salt can lose its savor, and Christians can be bearers of ugliness. In the following chapters we will attempt to define beauty and ugliness, look at some of the barriers to beauty, and explore the Church, God's divine beauty parlor.

Following our trip to the "beauty parlor," we will take a look at some exciting ways to show the world an alternative to paint and pillows.

Chapter 1

DEFINITION OF BEAUTY

The delightful movie *My Fair Lady* captured the hearts of millions of people around the world. The plot concerns Professor Higgins, the master of elocution, who made a wager with a friend that he could take an urchin off the streets and change her life by teaching her the principles of proper speech. Frivolous, impulsive, impish Eliza became the focus of his experiment. After months of effort (not without setbacks) a metamorphosis began to take place. A beautiful, polished, delicate, sophisticated young lady emerged from the cocoon of the formerly brazen, gauche girl of the streets.

The captivating story struck a responsive chord in nearly every heart because we all long for a Professor Higgins of some sort to wave a magic wand and make us beautiful. Somehow man suspects there is something better than the "paint and pillows" and so he waits on the lily pads of life for the liberating kiss of a beautiful princess. But is there really a princess running around looking for frogs in distress, or a professor who can transform lives with the magic of proper elocution? Ezekiel 16 answers that ques-

15

tion in the affirmative. It is a chapter of great hope because we are given answers that are rooted in reality and not fantasy. I suspect that the writers of "My Fair Lady" had read Ezekiel 16.

The passage could be entitled "My Fair Lady: from the Rubbish Heap to Royalty." In this chapter Ezekiel is instructed by God to remind the city of Jerusalem of her original condition and what God has done to make her beautiful. It's a wonderful story of God's love and grace set against the backdrop of Jerusalem's fickle heart. Let's observe God's words to Israel.

Rubbish Heap to Royalty

Scene One: *The Rubbish Heap*: Israel's tragic and humble beginning is set forth by the Lord in verses 3-5. "Your origin and your birth are from the land of the Canaanite, your father was an Amorite and your mother a Hittite. As for your birth, on the day you were born your navel cord was not cut, nor were you washed with water for cleansing; you were not rubbed with salt or even wrapped in cloths. No eye looked with pity on you to do any of these things for you, to have compassion on you. Rather you were thrown out into the open field, for you were abhorred on the day you were born" (NASB). Certainly the scene is not a happy one. Rejected by her parents, the baby (Israel) is thrown out into the field, unwashed and unloved. Death is inevitable. It is an ugly sight.

Scene Two: *The Rescue*: Every good story must have a rescue scene. This one is no exception! Verse 6 records it for us, "When I passed by you and saw you squirming in your blood, I said to you while you were in your blood, 'Live!'" (NASB). What a graphic description of God's grace! How thankful we should be that God loves the unlovely, rescues

16

those who are condemned to death. A hopeless, abandoned infant hears the call of God—an invitation to live and grow in the context of God's love. It is important to note at this point that it was man who relegated the newborn child to the rubbish heap. God is the one who takes that which is discarded by man as rubbish and makes it beautiful.

Scene Three: *The Romance*: What would a story be without a romance? Verse 7 describes the child's growth from infancy to adulthood. The little abandoned girl is now grown and ready for marriage. God responds in verse 8, "Then I passed by you and saw you, and behold, you were at the time for love; so I spread my skirt over you and covered your nakedness. I also swore to you and entered into a covenant with you so that you became mine" (NASB). *You became mine!* Somehow those words defy explanation. Taken dying from the rubbish heap, the infant child now becomes the bride of the King, the object of His love and devotion. What began with His invitation to live climaxes in a marriage—an invitation to love and be loved.

This same God has scheduled another wedding, for His Son, Jesus Christ. You and I, members of the body of Christ, are the bride. Christ pours out His love for us so that we may be presented to Him as a beautiful bride, not having spot or wrinkle (Eph. 5).

Scene Four: *Royalty*: Royalty—the impossible dream? Not when one becomes the bride of the King. When the King of Kings and Lord of Lords reaches down and draws that which is nothing to Himself, it is no longer nothing. Again, words are incapable of describing the wonder of it all. "You were exceedingly beautiful and advanced to royalty" (Ezek. 16:13b, NASB). What a pilgrimage: from the rubbish heap to royalty. What a revelation: God wants to pour out His resources to make His bride beautiful. His extravagance staggers the imagination.

"Then I bathed you with water, washed off your blood from you, and anointed you with oil. I also clothed you with embroidered cloth and put sandals of porpoise skin on your feet; and I wrapped you with fine linen and covered you with silk. And I adorned you with ornaments, put bracelets on your hands, and a necklace around your neck. I also put a ring in your nostril, earrings in your ears, and a beautiful crown on your head. Thus you were adorned with gold and silver, and your dress was of fine linen, silk and embroidered cloth. You ate fine flour, honey, and oil; so you were exceedingly beautiful and advanced to royalty" (Ezek. 16:9-14, NASB). This detailed passage conveys the strong impression that when God joins Himself to someone, He wants that person to be beautiful. Selah. Like it or not, we are scheduled to be masterpieces.

Scene Five: *Recognition*: You can't hide beauty. When God builds beauty into a person or nation, it will be recognized. "Then your fame went forth among the nations on account of your beauty, for it was perfect because of My splendor which I bestowed on you" (v. 14, NASB). The world listens when God is seen at work in human experience. In both the Old and New Testament, God's strategy has been to call forth a beautiful bride out of an ugly world. The infinite radiance of His beauty reflected through the person and work of the bride is designed to attract men to Him. We wait for Christ to return for His bride, the church. I've often wondered if the delay has anything to do with the ugliness of the bride.

God Is Our Source of Beauty

Salted away in the midst of this delightful account of God's beautification of Israel is an important statement of the nature and source of beauty. In verse 14 God states that Israel's beauty was "perfect because of My splendor which

I bestowed upon you" (NASB). Here we are taught that God is the source of beauty, and that He transfers His beauty to His creatures. The bride's beauty was the reflection of God's beauty. If this is true, *beauty is the possession and expression of the nature of God.* All believers possess the nature of God, but not all "express" it clearly. Peter tells us that we become "partakers of the divine nature" (II Pet. 1:4, KJV).

Beauty as a concept is not easy to define. It is part of the same family with truth, love, life, reality and holiness. These concepts are so closely tied together that one cannot speak of one without touching the other. Beauty will always be manifested where there is love, truth, unity, reality, etc. Where sin, darkness, falsehood, pretense, and death reign, ugliness will evidence itself. Relating beauty to such concepts as truth, love, and holiness presupposes an objective, universal standard. Not all agree that such a standard exists.

The Sawi Indians of New Guinea think Judas Iscariot is beautiful. They showed no response to the gospel until their missionary friend related the account of Christ's betrayal by Judas. Suddenly they came alive. Cheers and laughter filled the hut. Their applause was spontaneous and unrehearsed. They honor treachery as one of the highest virtues. Judas' skill in penetrating the "inner circle," gaining their complete confidence and then selling them out was viewed as a work of art, a masterpiece of deceit.[1]

But is treachery beautiful? Are we wrong in considering it to be ugly? Can it be both beautiful and ugly? Those who reject an objective standard for beauty, and claim that "beauty is in the eye of the beholder," feel that treachery can be ugly and beautiful. The Sawi Indians' preference for Judas over Jesus is simply a matter of personal choice.

---

[1]Don Richardson, *Peace Child* (Glendale, California: G/L Regal Books, 1974).

Beauty is subjective, and we must recognize that there are "different strokes for different folks." If you feel treachery is a vice, Judas is a villain. If it's a virtue, Judas is worthy of praise.

A much more satisfying approach to beauty suggests that it is really not important what the Sawi Indians felt about Judas' actions. Their subjective evaluation does not make betrayal beautiful or ugly any more than their personal preference makes a sunset beautiful or ugly. Accordingly, a rose is beautiful because it has attributes and qualities of beauty which it shares with every other truly beautiful thing. My perception of it as beautiful does not make it beautiful any more than my insensitivity to its beauty makes it ugly. This approach to beauty is based on an ultimate, infinite, objective standard revealed in Scripture. Treachery is evil, not because I feel it is, but because He who is holy called it such and declared that Judas was a devil (see John 6:70, 71).

An objective theory of beauty acknowledges the subjective element. The Bible reminds us that Rachel was beautiful and also talks about the beauty of holiness. The first is a statement about that which is *aesthetically* good and leaves room for subjectivity or personal preference. Who knows? You might have preferred weak-eyed Leah. The second description of beauty (holiness) deals with that which is *morally good*, and is not subjective. Beauty involves both the external and internal, the natural and the supernatural. Socrates believed that the one who wishes to become beautiful must begin with the internal disposition, or the soul. Given enough time, the beauty of the inner man would reflect itself in the appearance and actions of the outer or external man.

It has been said that "beauty is only skin deep, but ugliness goes all the way to the bone." But true beauty is not skin deep, it goes all the way to the soul. The major word for beauty in the greek language is *kalos*. It is often used to describe the outward form of an object. When used of a person it refers to that which is healthy, sound and organically whole. The person is *kalos* if he is pleasant, attractive, and creates a favorable sensory impression. When it is used of things, it can mean that which is organically healthy, fit, serviceable, and well adapted to its purpose. It is used to describe metal which is genuine, sterling or flawless. When used of a place, it refers to a suitable or convenient one. When used of a time, it denotes the right or appropriate time. When it is used of the inner disposition of man, it usually portrays that which is morally good.

Generally, however, the Greeks used *kalos* to describe the outward, external manifestations of *agathos*, or the "good." They recognized that behind the visible, observable *kalos*, was "invisible" *agathos*. Plotinus taught that the outward, visible manifestations of beauty in this world are simply reflections or specific illustrations of the *agathos*, the divine universal or unitary idea. What he is suggesting is that the *agathos*, the universal, takes form in the *kalos*, the particular. Scriptures tell us that only God is *agathos*. In Romans 7:18 Paul says "For I know that nothing good [*agathos*] dwells in me, that is in my flesh; for the wishing is present with me, but the doing of the good [*kalos*] is not" (NASB). The outward manifestations of goodness (beauty) are lacking because in his flesh (his old nature) dwells no good (*agathos*) thing. Because the universal, supernatural source of goodness is not present in the old nature, the old nature (the flesh) cannot produce *kalos*, or beauty. Therefore man must "possess" the good (the *agathos*) before he can do the good (*kalos*) or produce beauty.

Beauty is *the possession and expression of the nature of God*. The nonbeliever can produce beautiful objects and actions because he is an image bearer of God and even in his fallen state can reflect something of the creator's nature. God the Holy Spirit does convict him of sin, righteousness and judgment (see John 16:8). His conscience responding

21

to the truth of God reflected in societal laws and cultural expectations can direct him to do responsible, noteworthy things. Yet despite appearances to the contrary, if his nature is not changed through the new birth, the sum total of his life will not be beautiful. Underneath the "outward appearances" lies a heart that is deceitful and wicked. Only the new birth can change the inner man—the source of beauty or ugliness. It is well to point out that *not all that appears to be beautiful proves to be beautiful*. Man looks on the outward appearance, but God looks on the heart. If our inner man is going to be renovated, we must look to God who is the ultimate source and definition of beauty.

Expressions of God's Beauty

God's beauty is expressed in two key areas: in His *person* and in His *works*.

God is beautiful in His person. The English word "person" comes from the Greek word *prosopon* which is often translated "mask," something which covers the real person. Isn't it interesting that the very term used to describe man as a self-conscious, rational being reflects his inclination to run for the "paint and pillows." God too, is a person, yet not a "person" in the sense of one who covers, distorts and deceives. Instead, He is beautiful in His person, first of all, *because there is a direct correspondence between what He actually is and how He reveals Himself*. God possesses complete unity. Judas revealed himself as loyal, trustworthy and committed to the other disciples. They felt he was so much a part of them that they entrusted their finances to him. Yet there was no correspondence between what he claimed to be and what he actually proved to be.

About once a week I take my car to the car wash. After I pay for the car wash, I usually try to stand facing the car-washing machines. I know if I look in the other direction I will be staring at the candy machines. That's bad for me, because I have a terrible weakness for a particular candy bar. However, my mind wanders easily. I'm usually curious to know whether or not they still stock my favorite candy bar. I check. They do. Suddenly I find myself being carried to the candy bar machine by forces entirely beyond my control. Money somehow drops into the machine, a lever is pulled, and lo and behold, there it is, waiting patiently in the tray. At this point something ugly inevitably happens. I grab the bar, rip off its wrapper, and discover anew that the candy is about half the length of the cardboard bottom of the wrapper. In this world, what you see is not always what you get.

God is beautiful because there is a total unity between His internal disposition and His external appearance. He is the "same yesterday, today and forever" (see Heb. 13:8). Satan, the "angel of light," has the appearance of beauty, but as the "prince of darkness" does not possess the attributes of beauty. His external appearance is directly contradicted by his internal disposition. As the great deceiver, he goes through the world changing all the price tags, peddling rat poison disguised as bread. The scars of his deception have dulled our sensitivity to reality and truth, and often cause us to resist God's surgical procedures in our lives. What we want to hide, God wants to uncover; what we want to ignore, He wants to explore.

Part of developing beauty is realizing that beauty is based on a return to reality about ourselves. It is ugly to hide, cover, and distort truth, even if it is the truth about our inadequacy and failure. We do this because we have developed the mistaken idea that the revelation of inadequacy and failure is ugliness. Quite the opposite. One of the most moving scenes in human history could have been Judas confessing to Christ that he was plotting to kill Him, and seeking Christ's forgiveness. We are commanded to share our inadequacies and burdens, and this process can be a thing of beauty. The truth about our lives is that we are pilgrims destined to be like Him, yet in reality a long way from our destiny.

Second, God's person is beautiful *because His attributes lack nothing.* They have all the essential elements and as a result are flawless. They unite together in perfect harmony and balance. A flawless diamond not only has no impurities, but it is cut in such a way that makes maximum use of its ability to reflect light and beauty. To achieve such beauty, every angle, every facet must be perfect. Any flaw in one part diminishes the radiance of the whole. His love is perfect love, His justice is perfect justice, consequently He has *organic wholeness.* If you were to discover a severed hand lying on the pavement, it probably would create a strong sense of revulsion. Yet the hand is a marvel of engineering, a thing of beauty. Its beauty, however, grows out of its relationship and interdependence with the rest of the body. The body is not complete without a hand, and the hand is useless without the body. The body supplies the hand with vitality and significance. When both are present and functioning one beautifies and gives meaning to the other. Paul reminds us that a man can say the right things, have great knowledge, and even give his body to be burned, but if he does not have love, he is nothing and contributes nothing towards beauty (see I Cor. 13).

Scripture tells us that we are "complete in Him" (Col. 2:10, KJV). All that we need for life and God-like-ness is present in Him. Redemption provides us with the nature of God, and begins the process of expressing His nature through us. As His life begins to possess us and flow through us, we move toward organic wholeness because we are being set free to function according to divine specifications. He begins to cultivate all the essential attributes necessary to reflect Him accurately, that is, the fruits which belong to the Spirit.

Third, God's person is beautiful *because His attributes are perfectly balanced*. Each attribute of God is flawless, and links with the others in perfect harmony. He doesn't have too much of one quality and not enough of another. The Greek sculptor preferred the decathalon champion as his model because his body had symmetry and proportion. The nature of decathalon competition demanded the equal development of the entire body. The athlete had to be able to jump, run, and lift and throw weights. To develop excellence in the variety of athletic events, the athlete had to develop the potential of his entire body, and could not neglect one part without hurting his overall performance. When we speak of God as having balance, we mean He has just the right amounts of each essential quality. His justice is perfectly balanced by His love and holiness. God's being is characterized by a depth, a fulness and a glory beyond human comprehension. The Bible presents it as a glorious, harmonious whole without any inherent imbalance or contradictions.

Satan, however, is ugly because he is full of inconsistencies and contradictions. He has great wisdom, yet his rebellion against God will ultimately prove to be the epitome of foolishness. Claiming to give men wisdom, he is the father of lies. He knows only self-love even though he seems to be interested in the welfare of others.

We are marked by similar evidences of inconsistency and imbalance. The task-oriented, driving businessman who uses people to get the job done needs balance. His ability to accomplish things is both an asset and a liability. His greatest liability is often a lack of sensitivity to people and their needs. The warm, amiable, supportive person often lacks motivation and discipline. The calculating, analytical individual sometimes lacks social finesse and tends to appear cold and aloof. The expressive, social specialist sometimes has a tendency to be impulsive and anger prone. God's good news is that He has made provision to move us toward balance, symmetry and beauty.

We've seen that God's person is the source of beauty. He is beautiful because of His complete *unity and integrity*. There is a total and complete correlation between what He is and what He proves to be. We saw God's beauty reflected in the completeness and perfection of His attributes. All the essential qualities are fully present and flawless. These qualities are perfectly balanced so that no one quality dominates or creates imbalance. So far we have been talking about some of the attributes of God's being which help us define the essence of beauty. God's glorious person reveals itself through His works, and this dimension of His being is available for humans to observe and contemplate. The heavens declare His glory, and the earth reveals His craftsmanship. The incarnate Christ, the visible expression of the invisible God, is a living, visual aid of beauty in action.

The Beauty of God's Works

God's works are beautiful, first of all, *because His works are a true expression of what He is—His being*. Because God is infinite in wisdom, love, holiness, and so on, His works are beautiful. They find their origin in the being of one who is flawless. Our problem is one of credibility. We profess to believe one thing and practice something else. What God does is a perfect expression of what He is.

Second, God's works are beautiful *because they are the expression of one whose attributes are infinite*. What His perfect wisdom desires His infinite power can produce. Because of His flawless attributes, His plan is flawless. Because of His infinite power, His plan is invincible. What God wills will come to pass. This dimension of God is awesome in its glory and beauty. Those He called in eternity past will be glorified. Those He forgives will be forgiven. Those who trust Christ will go to that prepared place. Those who reject Christ will be separated from God for eternity. God's plan is beautiful because it embraces and explains all that comes to pass. It will successfully triumph against all opposition. In a limited sense, as we trust Him to enable us to overcome the inadequacies of our own lives our *progress* becomes a source of beauty. "To God be the glory, great things He hath done."

Scene 6: *Ruin*: There's one more scene to the drama of Ezekiel 16 which is not a part of *My Fair Lady*. It's a tragic reversal, an ugly pilgrimage back to the rubbish heap. The bride of God becomes a harlot, trampling the beauty of God in the dust. "But you trusted in your beauty and played the harlot because of your fame, and you poured out your harlotries on every passer-by who might be willing" (Ezek. 16:15, NASB). God's splendor was poured out on His bride, and she became beautiful, full of integrity, harmony and brightness. With her beauty came recognition, fame, and finally failure. The Lord gives five reasons why she lost her beauty.

First, *she trusted in her beauty, and forgot the God who made her beautiful*. In the limelight of fame she failed to give credit to the source of her beauty, and developed a misplaced trust. Pride filled her heart as people responded to what God had done in her, with the result that she misused the gift of God's beauty and eventually lost it.

Satan's downfall ran on similar tracks. In Ezekiel 28:12 God reminds us that in the beginning Satan was "full of wisdom and perfect in beauty" (NASB). Verses 13-15 go on to describe the magnificence of Satan's beauty. Verse 17 explains why he fell. "Your heart was lifted up because of your beauty; you corrupted your wisdom by reason of your splendor" (NASB). Pride is the great enemy of beauty. It leads one to believe that beauty is the possession and expression of his own nature instead of God's.

Second, the bride became a harlot *because of her fame*. Success is not easy to cope with. Beauty produced recognition, and recognition ruin. Ruin comes when we forget that we are His workmanship. He is the master craftsman, the source of all that is good. The more beauty we see in our lives the more thankful and dependent we should be.

Third, the bride prostituted herself *because she forgot to remember her pedigree*. "And besides all your abominations and harlotries you did not remember the days of your youth, when you were naked and bare and squirming in your blood" (Ezek. 16:22, NASB). How often we need to return to the foot of the cross and be reminded that He who was sinless became sin for us. God in His grace has lifted us up out of a horrible pit and put our feet on a rock. How easy it is to forget the rubbish heap when royalty and recognition come.

Fourth, the bride lost her beauty *because she neglected her heart*. Harlots have weak hearts. " 'How languishing [weak] is your heart,' declares the Lord God, 'while you do all these things, the actions of a bold-faced harlot' " (16:30, NASB). Beauty begins in the heart, and we must guard it with all diligence (see Prov. 4:23). Most of the ugliness seen in our lives is caused by heart trouble. We will develop this in a later chapter.

Fifth, she lost her beauty *because she associated with false lovers*. Because of her waywardness, God says that He will give her into the hands of her lovers who will "tear down your shrines, demolish your high places, strip you of your clothing, take away your jewels, and will leave you naked and bare" (Ezek. 16:39, NASB). When a person leaves the security of God's love for other lovers he soon discovers that man apart from God is an exploiter who tears down, demolishes, strips, takes and leaves. Satan has salted the earth with false lovers promising beauty but producing ugliness. God's love is designed to produce beauty. We will only know beauty as we allow God's love to work in our hearts unhindered.

Christ Is the Definition of Beauty

If beauty is the possession and expression of the nature of God, Jesus Christ is our living definition. As the visible expression of the invisible God (see Col. 1:15), all that He is and does is beautiful and becomes a model for us. In His life we see *unity*, a direct correspondence between His essential being and the way in which He reveals Himself. He proclaimed that the greatest demonstration of love is a man forfeiting His life for another—and He did. He taught that the great must be servant of all, and He washed His disciples' feet. He taught that a man should love his enemy, and prayed that His father would forgive His assassins.

His personality is flawless, having *proportion or harmony*. There are no overdeveloped, underdeveloped or missing qualities. His unbalanced disciples urged Him to send the children away, but He didn't. Peter urged Him to defend Himself in the garden, but He wouldn't. His enemies challenged Him to come off the cross if He was really God. He is God, but He didn't leave the cross. In Christ there is no impulsiveness, no hostility, not intolerance or bigotry. All His attributes blend together in perfect symmetry and proportion. He challenged the skeptics who rejected His person to believe because of His works (see John 10:37, 38). His works revealed the glory and splendor of His person.

The good news is that our destiny is to be like Him. To make that a reality, God is extending an invitation to us to live and to grow, to possess His nature and then express it. Possession begins with the new birth (John 3:1-16). Expression of His nature begins by allowing His love to work in our lives to call forth beauty. The rest of the book is designed to help us see some of the practical steps necessary to moving from the "Rubbish heap to Royalty."

Chapter 2

COSMETICS OF THE HEART

The English word "cosmetics" comes from the Greek word *kosmos* which means "to make order out of chaos." Let's face it, the cosmetic industry flourishes because most of us look like "chaos" at 6:30 a.m. As the flush of youth dims, the rush for cosmetic camouflage begins. Our culture worships youthfulness and cosmetics help veil its passing. My pastor used to remind us that "a little red paint never hurt a barn." Although a coat of red paint may give a barn a new lease on life, drug store cosmetics cannot create beauty out of the chaos within the human heart. Beauty certainly involves outward form, but the secret to beauty does not lie in a tube of this or a bottle of that. True beauty is not skin deep; it goes all the way to the heart. Unfortunately, the heart is beyond the reach of this world's cosmetics. Sin has created an eternal heartache which temporal bicarbonates cannot ease.

The heart of man is pictured in Scripture as the center of the rational-spiritual nature of man. It is the seat of love and hatred, thought and conception, feelings and affection. The heart is that part of us which experiences joy, sorrow, anxiety and pain. It is the center of our moral life, the

31

place of origin of all that is good and evil in thoughts, words and actions. The heart becomes the place of God's residence in us when we respond to His grace. God says that the natural condition of man's heart is not good, in fact, it is "deceitful above all things, and desperately wicked" (Jer. 17:9, KJV). Man's spiritual ecology is pretty grim. The pollution of his heart works outward, prostituting his personality and relationships.

Band-aids won't suffice. Man needs the radical intervention of God to be beautiful. Nothing short of a miracle can bring beauty to man's heart. Thank God He's not short on miracles. Paul describes the wonder of God's provision to his friend Timothy, pastor of the church in Ephesus. "The ultimate aim of the Christian minister, after all, is to produce the love which springs from a pure heart, a good conscience and a genuine faith" (I Tim. 1:5, Phillips). God is love, and we are in the ministry for the purpose of helping each other possess and reflect that priceless attribute. Paul doesn't say that the ultimate aim of our instruction is to make everyone premillennial dispensationalists, or supralapsarians. The goal of it all is love. It is the distinguishing beauty mark of the believer. Is there anything more beautiful than the love of a mother for a baby, a husband for a wife, a boy for his dog?

Timothy was surrounded by teachers proclaiming a philosophy of life which led to endless discussions and questions for which they had no answers. Not only did their teaching lead to futility, but, Paul says, it contradicted God's provisions for man's dilemma, provisions which operate on the basis of faith. God's provision for the beautification of man is to rewire his heart, his conscience and his manner of life. Serious car lovers often pull a brand new engine out of a car and have it "blue printed." To blueprint an engine means to machine it to exact factory specifications. The goal of such a process is an engine which runs exactly as designed. Because we have "blown the blue-

32

print," we need to be restored to divine specifications if we are to reflect the beauty of the designer.

Obstacles to Beauty

Note that God's provision confronts three major obstacles: an impure heart, a guilt-ridden conscience and a life of pretense. Love, and therefore beauty, is virtually eliminated from the life of man when these qualities prevail. If my heart is impure, it *contaminates* the expression of God's love and my conscience becomes laden with guilt. A guilty conscience *confines* the expression of love, and encourages me to run for the paint and pillows. A life of pretense *counterfeits* love and robs it of its beauty and power. The net result is ugliness which even the paint and pillows cannot hide.

The pilgrimage to beauty begins with the heart. A few years ago I was able to visit the Strategic Air Command headquarters in Nebraska. We were taken five stories underground to the command post where decisions are made and orders sent which affect the destiny of the entire world. It was an awesome experience to be at the very nerve center of a vast military network stretching around the globe. Our hearts are like that command post. Proverbs 4:23 commands man to "watch over your heart with all diligence, for from it flow the springs of life" (NASB). This verse reminds us that the heart's condition determines the outcome of the life.

Matthew records Christ's description of the tragic harvest of a polluted heart. "But the things that proceed out of the mouth come from the heart, and those defile the man. For out of the heart come evil thoughts, murders, adulteries, fornications, thefts, false witness, slanders. These are the things which defile the man . . ." (Matt. 15:18-20, NASB).

Look at the list again—wall to wall ugliness. Where does it come from? The heart. A polluted heart produces a poisoned mind, which produces a prostituted body and a poisoned tongue. Inner pollution destroys purity, blocks intimacy, destroys the beauty of sex and shuts down significant relationships. Jonathan Edwards said that "the heart is like a viper hissing and spitting poison at God." How true! An impure heart is a malignancy which infects everything it touches.

Out of the heart come evil thoughts. We all struggle with evil thoughts during our pilgrimage toward glory. Such thoughts not only damage our own walk with the Lord, but are the source of much pain in human relationships. How we feel is often the product of how we think. Remember what it was like when you were smitten with "puppy love"? The world was a wonderful place, everything seemed to be dipped in stardust. Your sweetheart was bigger than life, a dream come true, a "many splendored thing." Your emotions were in overdrive, short circuiting all reality and common sense. Why? Because your thoughts about your sweetheart were all positive. You saw her or him at her or his best.

The emotional period of ecstatic paralysis began to disappear as soon as reality began to filter through the fantasy. You began to see and think about some of the person's shortcomings, and the emotional tempest in a teapot began to lose its steam. In marriage there is often a complete reversal of perspective and with that a reversal of affection.

After the honeymoon is over, it is common to lock in on the negative to such an extent that we poison our emotional structure and lose our love. There is a direct correlation between how we think and how we feel. Yet according to I Corinthians 13 love keeps no record of wrongs, and does not delight in evil. A pure heart focuses upon and encourages that which is pure, and as a result establishes a context in which love is free to grow in spite of personal inadequacies.

The Lord mentions that adulteries and fornications are the results of an impure heart. Both sins are especially ugly because they prostitute not only bodies but personalities. In most cases the other person is viewed as a bearer of function rather than a being. An evil heart motivates us to fall in love with the package and not the contents. All of us are susceptible to such temptations and must guard our hearts with all diligence lest we succumb.

"Thefts" is another product of impurity, according to our Lord. Stealing of any kind is wrong, but stealing one's reputation is much more costly than stealing his color TV set.

Taking anything from another is the product of impurity, whether it be his possessions, his personality or his reputation.

The final two products our Lord lists are false witnesses and slanders. Here he describes one of the most painful experiences the human being perpetrates upon another human. To be the victim of slanders, lies and false testimony is one of life's most painful experiences. It's to be trapped and to have little hope of recourse. Our Lord ends his discussion by reminding us that it is the products of an impure heart which defile the life and personality of man. Paul reminds us that love cannot co-exist with impurity. Beauty and impurity are mutually exclusive.

Steps to Beauty

Thank God there is a solution to pollution! The word "pure" in I Timothy 1:5 gives us our first clue to becoming beautiful. It should be translated "cleansed." The first step toward beauty is *conversion*—the washing of regeneration, the new birth. The shed blood of Christ is God's only cleansing agent for the heart. Only His work on the cross makes purity possible. The very word "cleansed" presupposes dirt.

The first step toward conversion is to acknowledge impurity. We know from medicine that an accurate diagnosis is fundamental to cure. This means that each person must take inventory of his life and face ugliness and sin with integrity.

The second step toward conversion is a pilgrimage to the foot of the cross. Its shadow must fall across my life. I must see a Saviour dying in my place, bearing my ugliness and in its place offering me the gift of life and purity.

The third step is repentance. I must turn from the old and embrace the new. I must respond to His offer of forgiveness and receive Him into my heart as its new Lord and master. Receiving Him by faith makes me His son, a possessor of his nature. This conversion is the first step in the pilgrimage from the rubbish heap to royalty.

The second step toward beauty is *consecration*. Redemption (conversion) buys me out of the slave market of sin, and assures me I will never again be sold into slavery. But this does not mean I cannot go back to the slave market and be engaged again in the business of my old master. Redemption assures me that I no longer have to be enslaved to the evil one. I am free to grow in grace and godliness. To do this I must resist the allure of the old life and learn new attitudes and actions which reflect the nature of God. Napoleon said that "a man becomes the man of his uniform." If change is going to take place, I must visualize clearly the kind of person God wants me to become, and then determine by an act of the will, by a commitment, to become that kind of person.

It involves presenting myself to Him as an instrument for righteousness (see Rom. 6:13), as a living sacrifice (see

Rom. 12:1), and a vessel for honor (see II Tim. 2:21). If we aim at nothing, we'll hit it every time. We become what we conceive ourselves to be. Beauty comes from discovering God's blueprint for our lives, and making a commitment to pursue it with total dedication.

Beauty is expensive. Only those willing to pay the cost will reap the benefits. There is a direct correlation between beauty and consecration. Consecration is not simply a commitment to be, but to do. There are disciplines which are necessary if we are to grow in grace and beauty. If we are to be like Him, we need to commune with Him. Our lives must be permeated with truth, and truth will produce beauty. You know what I am going to say: daily devotions and prayer. Right! Set aside regular time for fellowship with Him. Make it the first priority of each day. Share this desire with another brother in Christ, and let him help you implement it by holding you accountable. Meditation upon truth is a key to beauty.

The third step toward beauty is *confession*. When our thoughts stray into forbidden territory, when our emotions boil over, when our motivations become self-centered, we need cleansing. We long for that day when we will be delivered from the power and presence of sin. Until then, we must wrestle with its influence on a moment by moment basis. Unfortunately, we don't always walk by means of the Spirit of God, we don't always avail ourselves of His provisions for victory over temptation. When we sin we must deal with it. Confession is the prerequisite to cleansing and restoration of fellowship. Confession means "to say the same thing." When we say what God says about the impurity which crops up in our hearts, he promises to forgive, cleanse and forget (see I John 1:9). God's beautiful people have instituted an effective preventive maintenance program. They guard their hearts with all diligence. They know that the fabric of their lives is woven from what is put into their hearts. It only takes a pinch of sand to ruin a cake, a little impurity to soil a relationship, a minor leak to sink a ship. Life is both sugar and strychnine. If someone hands me a cup of coffee with strychnine in it, it doesn't make any difference if he's a friend or foe. The results are the same. Beautiful people stand guard at the door to their hearts and do not allow anyone, friend or foe, to dump garbage in it.

Do you want to be beautiful? God wants you to be beautiful. His blueprint begins with your *conversion*. Only His presence can produce beauty, and He comes into our hearts by faith. Following conversion, God wants us to bring ourselves to Him in total *consecration*. This consecration involves cultivating purity by filling our lives with positive wholesome, beautiful things—most of which come from His Word. *Confession* is necessary when we allow impure thoughts, actions and attitudes to intrude into our lives.

If you were to heap up the contents of your heart and give it to a friend, would he be happy with what he received, or would he spend all morning sifting garbage? Only God can make order out of chaos. His process begins with the cosmetics of the heart. Conversion, consecration and confession keep it functioning as God designed, and everything He designs is beautiful.

Chapter 3

A CLEAR CONSCIENCE

Once a year the town drunk made a pilgrimage to the church to settle the score with his creator. His usual pattern was to stumble down the aisle praying "Lord, clean out the cobwebs, clean out the cobwebs." One old lady, exasperated by the drunk's routine, interrupted his trip to the altar by standing and praying "Lord, forget the cobwebs, kill the spider."

Paul is "killing spiders" when he reveals in I Timothy that love and beauty find their source in a pure heart. Any approach to beauty that attempts to bypass the heart is simply cleaning out cobwebs. Although love flows only from a cleansed heart, God's cosmetic surgery must also touch the conscience if wholeness is to be ours. This is true because the heart and conscience exist together in a cause-effect relationship. They are so closely linked together that they catch each other's diseases. An impure heart produces a guilt-ridden conscience.

So what is the conscience? At times, the conscience is a red warning light on our spiritual dashboard which tells us that something is wrong with the heart. At other times it is a spiritual magnetic north pole which assures us that we are navigating within the boundary conditions of God's character. Sometimes it is a red light, and other times a green light. Someone has said that the conscience is that part of me which feels bad when everything else feels good. We can all identify with that.

The IRS received a letter from a conscience-stricken tax-payer. It said, "Dear Sir: My conscience bothered me. Here is the $175.00 which I owe in back taxes." There was a P.S. at the bottom which read, "If my conscience still bothers me, I'll send in the rest." This taxpayer's response to a red warning light is not only humorous, it illustrates an important truth: our consciences can become insensitive. Paul tells us that it can become "seared" or weak (see I Tim. 4:2).

Let's think about what happens when we put tape over the red warning light. The flashing light is a protective mechanism reminding us to take corrective actions before serious damage is done. Any type of impurity triggers it and calls for an immediate resolution. If we ignore it, the impurity of heart produces guilt, and unresolved guilt reinforces the lifestyle of a fugitive. So what do I do? I build Berlin walls between myself and others. Guilt confines the expression of love. Imagine yourself as an IRS agent living next door to a chronic tax violator. Even if you had no knowledge of your neighbor's prodigal tax returns, it's unlikely you could build a significant relationship with him. His guilt would make such a relationship impossible. We're told that "perfect love casts out fear" (I John 4:18, NASB). The reverse is also true: fear casts out love—it precludes it.

Paul tells Timothy that love flows from a good or "clear" conscience. A clear conscience is an inner freedom of spirit which comes from knowing that no one is able to point a finger at me and accuse me of wrongs I have not made right. A clear conscience is absolutely necessary if I am to be a bearer of beauty. Paul told Timothy that a clear conscience was his second most important weapon. Timothy was sent out "to battle for the right armed only with your faith and a *clear conscience*. Some, alas, have laid these simple weapons contemptuously aside and as far as their faith is concerned, have run their ships on the rocks" (I Timothy 1:18, 19, Phillips, italics added).

In Psalm 32, David graphically pictures the effects of a guilty conscience on one's physical body. Unresolved guilt produces all kinds of psychosomatic illnesses. The writer to the Hebrews reveals to us that the mature man is one who has developed a sensitive conscience (the ability to discriminate between good and evil; see Heb. 5:13, 14). There is a direct correlation between the condition of my conscience and my ability to witness, my effectiveness in resisting temptation, my ability to make wise decisions and my capacity to develop significant friendships.

God's Provision for Guilt

What excites me is that there is good news to proclaim! God's provision includes all that is necessary to deal with our guilt and usher us into the joyous freedom of a clear conscience. For many, however, guilt is like a boomerang—they don't know how to throw it away.

The story of the prodigal son gives us our model for gaining a free conscience (see Luke 15:11-32). After he spent his inheritance he found himself destitute in a pig pen. Here the bubble burst, and he came to his senses. He realized his father's servants were better off than he, and determined to return home and sign on as a servant. When he arrived home he had two very important things to say to his dad. First, he said, "I've sinned against God." Second, "I've sinned against you." He acknowledged his guilt and sought forgiveness from *both God and man*.

When I was a student in college I cheated on some quizzes. The red warning light went on, and I felt horrible. I tried to alleviate the guilt by purposely putting down wrong answers on subsequent quizzes. My cheating actually didn't help me grade-wise because I "made it right." The "light" didn't go off. I asked God to forgive and thanked Him for forgiveness. The "light" stayed on. Maybe I didn't confess hard enough. So I'd confess again to no avail. Finally I told the Lord "OK, I'll tell the professor." I went into his office and we chatted about all kinds of things except the issue. The bell rang. He picked up his books to go to class. I blurted it out. He forgave. The light went out.

While in high school I treated a girlfriend in a very cruel manner. I was immature and didn't know how to end a relationship. My motto was "Rush'em, mush'em, crush'em, flush'em!" And so I did.

Back on the farm we had a tractor with a quirk. Sometimes after we worked it hard for several hours we would shut off the key but the tractor would keep on running. We soon learned that the best way to stop it was to drive it against a tree, turn off the key, and let out the clutch. It stopped!

Nobody ever showed me how to end a relationship any more gracefully than our method for stopping that tractor. I was not a negotiator. When it was over, it was over. Period.

My actions toward that former girlfriend bothered me for years. Whenever I'd tell the Lord I wanted to be His man, I wanted my life to count for Him, this girl would be brought to my attention. I had asked the Lord for forgiveness again, but the red light stayed on. Finally I said "OK, Lord, if I ever see her again, I'll ask her to forgive me." Small chance, she was at least 1100 miles away. Shortly thereafter I found myself in a small rural church, looked up into the choir, and you guessed it, there she was. I knew what I had to do, and painful as it was, I asked her forgiveness and she granted it. The light went out. We've been good friends ever since.

In Matthew 5:23-24 our Lord tells us that even if we're bringing a sacrifice to the altar, if we have offended a brother our first responsibility is to make that relationship right. The sacrifice can come later.

But we've hurt many people; how can we make all these wrongs right? God seems to know how much pride we need to swallow, how many difficult confrontations are necessary to bring us to a point of humility and dependence upon Him. It's almost as though the Holy Spirit takes a big dip net and runs it through our past. He brings up certain people and circumstances which need to be healed and designs a pilgrimage to wholeness around what He chooses to bring up. He knows just how many wrongs we must make right to enable us to walk long enough on "Humble Street."

The first step toward freedom of conscience is to invite the Spirit of God to reactivate your memory so that you can list those from whom you need to gain forgiveness. We need the Spirit's assistance because we tend to suppress bad memories. Ask yourself some of the following questions: 1. To whom have I lied? 2. From whom have I stolen? 3. Who has been a victim of my temper? 4. Toward whom am I bitter, refusing to forgive? 5. Against whose authority have I rebelled? 6. Whose reputation have I damaged by slander or gossip?

Second, assign some kind of priority to the list of offenses. Having done this, deal with those of major importance first. The ones we have offended most should be dealt with first. You will discover an amazing fact as God leads you to ask forgiveness. He often makes it easier than you expect.

Third, think through carefully what you intend to say *before* you ask forgiveness. Your request for forgiveness should include an honest, brief description of the basic sin without dredging up unnecessary details, yet without minimizing it. Your request must reflect genuine repentance and humility. You must seek forgiveness, expecting nothing in return.

Fourth, expect a battle. Pride dies hard. Excuses will multiply geometrically. We are masters at rationalizations.

Excuses to Avoid

The following excuses are to be avoided; they are not legitimate reasons for putting off doing it.

1) "Things have improved." This may be true, but it does not negate the necessity of gaining a clear conscience. If things are better, it should be easier to seek forgiveness. Do it!

2) "It happened years ago; why dredge up the past?" If time erases, why do you remember it so vividly when you would like to forget it? It's a barrier to the flow of God's love. Deal with it!

3) "It's such an insignificant offense." Really? Then why does it keep coming up? If it's been weighing upon your conscience it is big enough to take care of.

4) "Everyone makes mistakes." True, yet the fact that you are bothered by it indicates that you have violated your own standards and need to make it right.

5) "It will only make matters worse." Perhaps. But obedience to God involves risks. It is important to separate the decision-making process from the problem-solving process. My decision to obey God and ask forgiveness created lots of problems. If we anticipate the problems obedience creates, and allow them to overwhelm us, we probably won't obey God. Obey God, and trust Him to solve the problems obedience creates.

I personally believe that the humiliating pride-swallowing process of asking forgiveness is the fee to be "paid" in God's beauty parlor. It's often costly, but you're never the same once it has been paid. A great sense of freedom, of release, of joy, of spiritual vitality seems to flow from honest confession and forgiveness. I found my pilgrimage through the land of "guilty conscience" to be difficult, yet rewarding beyond my greatest expectation. It has enabled me to be more real, more approachable and more effective in communicating with others.

Guilt is the burden of an unpaid debt. It's a beauty killer. Want to be beautiful? How about inviting God to perform a white glove inspection of your heart, and then take whatever steps are necessary to make that red warning light go out. Don't pray that He will "clean out the cobwebs." Kill the spider! Do it. You'll sleep better, and be more beautiful too!

Chapter 4

LIFE WITHOUT PRETENSE

A young boy was asked, "What is the chief aim of man?" by the instructor of his confirmation class. Without hesitation he replied, "Man's chief aim is to glorify God and annoy Him forever." Annoy Him forever . . . how often we *feel* that way.

Although the boy's answer was wrong, it contains volumes of truth. I either "glorify God" or I "annoy Him." Perhaps "displease" Him would be a better term. So what does it mean to "glorify" God? To give glory to God is not to add something that is missing, but to acknowledge something that is there. The glory of God is the dignity and value of His attributes. Life offers us two alternatives. We either seek to call attention to our own "glory," or we reveal the glory of the creator. To possess "glory" means to have something which is so weighty and impressive that it demands respect. Paul says we have it in a clay pot. We have a glorious treasure in an earthen vessel (see II Cor. 4:7). We have the indwelling presence of God in our human bodies. We possess the very nature of an all glorious God! Think of it. So why do we spend most of our lives shining the pot? Two options: shine the pot and conceal the glory of God, or break the pot and reveal the glory of God.

Paul told Timothy that love and beauty flow from a heart that is pure, a conscience that is clear, and a life that is free of hypocrisy (see I Tim. 1:5). Hypocrisy is the tip of the iceberg. You can't see my heart or my conscience, but you can see my lifestyle. The Lord told the Pharisees that they were like tombs painted white. They made an attempt to appear "OK" on the outside, but were full of corruption on the inside. A white washed grave—what a travesty. No clever arrangement of rotten eggs will make a good omelet.

The Pharisees provide us with a good example of "empty pot painters."

Proclaiming "truth" they produced ugliness. Originally the Pharisees were a lay movement whose goal was to bring the lifestyle of the priest into everyday life. When the priests served before the altar, there was a great concern about purity and lack of defilement. They performed numerous washings and other rituals of purification to assure their freedom from uncleanness. The Pharisees translated these priestly functions into the affairs of daily life. They came to view themselves as the representatives of the holy and pure community of "true Israel." They were the "blue bloods," in contrast to the "people of the land" whom they disdained and considered uncouth.

To become a Pharisee, a "keeper of the law," was an involved process. The candidate had to demonstrate he could protect himself from all defilement. He must be able to successfully guard his clothes from even being touched by the "people of the land." He could have no fellowship with them. Above all, he must never accept their hospitality or extend it to them. Conducting business with them was strictly forbidden. To give a daughter in marriage to one from the "people of the land" was considered as bad as giving her over to a wild beast.

The Talmud describes seven classes of Pharisees. I will mention four of them. First, the "shoulders" Pharisee. This person wears his good deeds on his shoulders for all to see. Second, the "wait a little" Pharisee begs for time in order to perform a meritorious action . . . all for show, of course. Third, the "bleeding Pharisee" who spots a beautiful woman, and in his eagerness to avoid looking on her with lust, closes his eyes and so bruises himself by running into the wall. Finally, the "painted Pharisee" who advertises his holiness to warn the "unclean" against touching and defiling him.

It's not surprising they criticized Christ for eating with unclean hands, for associating with the "dregs" of society.

When I was a young child I lived in mortal fear of a great aunt who was forever threatening to "box my ears in." I wasn't sure what she meant, but her massive body convinced me that whatever it was, she was fully capable of doing it. Religion is like that. It's always an attempt to corral another steer or box in another life. Religion demands uniformity because it has no unity. Praise God that because we have Him, we have unity, and as a result we don't have to be the same.

In chapter one we referred briefly to Christ's encounter with the Pharisees over the issue of fasting. Let's look at it in a little more detail.

The Pharisees fasted two days each week, and Christ didn't. They wanted to "box Him in" to their expectations. They were upset because Jesus allowed His disciples to do "secular" things on a "sacred" day. Christ replied by using two powerful illustrations which help us understand the freedom and creativity which we have in Christ. The Lord reminded the Pharisees that no rational person would sew a new piece of cloth onto an old garment because the new cloth would shrink and tear it. Likewise, no rational person would put new, unfermented wine into an old wineskin because the pressures of fermentation would cause it to burst (see Mark 2:21, 22). So what's the big idea? Christ is introducing a new lifestyle so radical that it cannot function within the old forms. He did not come to add new pieces to an old garment. He did not come to put new wine into used wineskins.

The Leaven of the Pharisees

Christ came to proclaim a new relationship which requires new expressions. So why bring up the Pharisees? Because they were "keepers of the old wineskins." Their motto was "Never on the Sabbath." In Matthew 16 Christ warns against allowing their leaven, and hypocrisy, to permeate our lives and produce *ugliness* (see v. 6). They were fruit inspectors, continually seeking to demonstrate their purity by separating themselves from "sinners." They established spiritual "pecking orders" based on external performance rather than inner qualities.

One cannot help but chuckle as he reflects on some of their "wineskins." These were some of their rules for the Sabbath. It was OK to spit on a rock, but not in the dirt, because to spit in the dirt made mortar, and that was work. If a wall fell on some unlucky soul on the Sabbath, you were allowed to clear away only enough rubble to determine his condition. If he was dead, you had to leave him until the Sabbath was over. If he was alive, you could dig him out. If his leg was fractured, he had to bite a bullet because no aid could be rendered on the Sabbath. A cut finger could be bandaged, but you couldn't put any ointment on it until after the Sabbath. You were allowed to ride a donkey on the Sabbath, but you couldn't carry a switch because this laid a burden upon the donkey, and that was work! The Talmud talks about pious Rabbinic mules which refused to eat untithed corn on the Sabbath. We could go on and on. Try-

50

ing so hard to be beautiful, to be right, to be pure, and the Son of God labels them as total phonies. Pure ugliness!

Were there cracks in the pots of the Pharisees? Certainly! Were there impurities in the pots of the Pharisees? Certainly! Are there cracks in my pot? Impurities? Weaknesses? Certainly. Are they beautiful? No. Can they be beautiful? Not if I hide them. To have cracks, flaws and weaknesses is *not* the problem. Where two or three pots are gathered together, there are cracks in their midst. The hypocrites hide them, the healthy acknowledge them.

Some of our flaws are blameworthy. That is, we have them because we have allowed impurity to bring forth its harvest. All the Pharisees fled when invited to throw stones at the adulterous woman. Why? Because Christ saw beyond the paint and pillows, and invited those who were innocent of adultery to be her executioners. For some, the first step towards a life of transparency and beauty is confession of sin to both God and man.

Other flaws are not the result of moral failure, but simply reflect the present state of our pilgrimage. These "flaws" are capacities not yet fully developed, skills not yet fully mastered, abilities not yet matured. Many Christians are trying to let their "perfection" be known to all men, and as a result attempt to disguise or cover their inadequacies.

Every other Thursday for over two years I have been having lunch with a brother in Christ named Dick Underwood. Dick has a camper which he drives to work. This camper has become a "chapel on wheels." Dick has fixed lunch for me in that camper dozens of times. We share together, we study God's word, and we pray together. Both of us have profited greatly by this experience and look forward, Lord willing, to many years of continued fellowship. Dick is a tremendously gifted man, and yet he is unconvinced of his potential. The exciting thing is seeing it begin to unfold. He's now teaching a home Bible class, speaking to various groups, and meeting regularly with other men in

SECRETS TO INNER BEAUTY

his "chapel on wheels." Dick's growth spurt can be traced back almost to the day that he came out from behind his facade and began to share honestly and openly concerning his life, his dreams, goals, fears and aspirations. Dick, his wife Tula, and I just returned from speaking at a four day conference. Dick had the last session and did an outstanding job. It was an incredible risk for a shy, introverted man. But Tula and I saw a new Dick in action. He made a great effort to mix with people and be open to their needs. God used him in a remarkable way because he was open and vulnerable.

The Biblical pattern is "let your *progress* be made known to all men." Progress implies imperfection. Dick shared his fear of speaking when he got up and spoke. The people understood, and responded with love and encouragement.

Help from God's Beauty Parlor

The body of Christ is God's divine beauty parlor, and He has salted it with people who are strong in areas of my weakness. If I struggle with organizing my affairs, God has plenty of gifted people who can be of help to me. If you struggle with financial matters, God has gifted people available. If your Achilles' heel is your children, God has resource people who can provide counsel and help. There is only one prerequisite to tapping a vast wealth of resources: you must give others the gift of your need. For many Christians, (especially pastors) this is a new skill to learn, a new risk to take. Not to do it is to say "I am an eye, and I have no need of the hand" (see I Cor. 12:21). Paul had a lot to say about those kind of people, and it wasn't good. We are members of one another, and are to bear one another's burdens, as Dick has borne mine. He has been a real source of strength and encouragement to me as I struggle in my walk with the Lord.

Another type of "flaw" is a constitutional one—a physical or emotional handicap which limits us in some way. I have a "weakness" which is a source of great embarrassment to me. I call it my "Jeremiah syndrome." Sometimes when I am speaking, I get misty eyed, choke up and generally make a fool of myself. I don't know why I do it, and furthermore, I have no desire to do it. But I can't control it, and it never happens unless I'm "surrounded by witnesses." I've asked God many times to remove it, but He hasn't. Paul also had a "weakness" which he asked God to remove, but instead of answering his request God revealed the great secret that His strength is made perfect in our weakness. Paul concluded that if God's glory shines from the platform of his weakness, then he would *glory in his weakness* (see II Cor. 12:9). To glory in something is to acknowledge something that is there. Instead of allowing physical and emotional limitations to produce bitterness and resentment, Paul's secret is thanksgiving. Beautiful people are thankful people, who acknowledge weakness and praise God because through that crack the glory of God can shine.

Are you a pot painter? Give it up. Join the thousands who are discovering that God is not at war with their humanity. God desires that we have integrity when what we feel and what we think is expressed in what we do. If we maintain a pure heart and conscience, our thoughts and feelings will be positive and beautiful. When this is true, what we are and do will reveal the beauty of an infinite God. What an exciting challenge!

Chapter 5

THE POSTURE OF BEAUTY

"Humpty Dumpty was pushed!" I can fully identify with the unknown street philosopher who expressed his sentiments in writing on a downtown wall. Not only was he pushed, but his "fall" produced amnesia . . . he doesn't know who he is. Most of us grow up feeling like a post-fall Humpty-Dumpty. We're a splattered, battered pile of pieces being assembled by an indifferent horde of the "King's men." Each "King's man" brings to us a bit of information about ourselves from which we try to assemble the pieces of our "Who in the World am I?" puzzle. Like it or not, our personalities are products of the relationships we have sustained.

Mrs. Martin illustrates our dilemma. Sick in bed with the flu, she received a "get well card" from her fourth grade class. Beneath the rosy printed "card company" sentiment was a note from her class which expressed theirs: "Dear Mrs. Martin, your fourth grade class wishes you a speedy recovery by a vote of 15 to 14." It's funny, and probably apocryphal, yet we can all identify with Mrs. Martin's experience. Most of us have wandered as lost souls in search of definition. Who am I? Why am I here? Where am I going? In our quest for definition, our search for a reference point which will give meaning to the particulars of life, the data we gather usually comes from the opinions, reactions and feedback of others involved in the same quest. As we allow them to define our sense of meaning and worth, we inadvertently become their victims. The insecure mother who becomes emotionally unzipped when her darling infant cries "I hate you!" is a case in point.

Beauty is the possession and expression of the nature of God. He alone is the ultimate source of definition, and we will only be beautiful as we live within the framework of His definition. Unfortunately by the time many of us come to know the Saviour and finally grasp the truths of His definition, we are the victims of reams of misinformation. I was no exception. So who is Joe Aldrich? The answer to that question would depend upon when you took the snapshot. Joe Aldrich the high school and college student would have tried very hard to convince you that he was an athlete, scholar, student leader and lover. During these formative years, my definition would have focused around those roles or images I worked hard at perpetuating. I would want you to know I was an "athlete" lettering in two sports, a "scholar" graduating near the top of my high school class, and first in my college class. In seminary I graduated with honors and won three faculty awards. Don't stop now, it gets worse. I worked hard to be elected student body vice-president and campaigned for and won several other positions in student government. My senior class voted me its "outstanding personality."

Another role I worked hard at perpetuating was the image of a "lover." I felt important when surrounded by admiring girls and I generally pursued the ones who aided my "role" as an important person. Athlete, scholar, student leader, lover—so who cares. There is nothing more pathetic than a person trying to live on faded press clippings and

56

frayed lettermen's sweaters. For me, these roles were simply window dressing by which I hoped to win respect, and perhaps admiration.

But who was the "real" Joe Aldrich living behind these roles? I was an insecure, fearful young person who often used sarcastic humor to keep people from getting too close. I was faculty editor of our student annual, and yet so insecure that when "annual signing" time came I ran around in sheer panic. I'm sure you remember those days, with everyone rushing to get their annuals signed. We all wanted more than an autograph. We really wanted a glowing (and usually apocryphal) description of how wonderful we were. Especially prized was a signature from one of the beautiful people. A personal note from such a one was clear proof to everybody of your significance and value. So what do you do if you're so insecure that you're afraid to ask some of the "heavies," the "beautiful people," to sign your annual? You do what I did—sign it yourself. That's right, you fake their signatures and try to impress others by how many people consider you a "friend."

These identity crises are not limited to teenagers. Our adult population is riddled with people still playing these identity games. Each spring an interesting set of such games was "scheduled" between the teachers and the painters of the Dallas Independent School District. When the spring semester ended at the seminary, I signed on with the painters, trading my "graduate student hat" for a painter's white hat, shirt and pants. The uniform was mandatory and became our identifying sign—we were painters.

The teachers, unimpressed by our "painters' whites," were less than enthusiastic about our arrival at their school. I suppose I'd be upset too if I were trying to wring some value out of the last days of school and my efforts were frustrated by painters chipping, scraping, and painting in my classroom. That we took our breaks in the teachers' lounge seemed to be the ultimate blow. Not only had we violated the sacredness of the classroom, but we invaded their inner sanctum with reckless abandon. With apologies to the painting profession, these representatives of the trade did leave much to be desired. Their reputation as somewhat less than wholesome citizens was not overly exaggerated. However, I discovered that the teachers were suffering from "hardening of the categories," and I became a victim of their pigeonholing mentality. Because I wore the uniform of the painter, I was entitled to all the rights and privileges which went with it. One such "right" was to be declared "guilty by association." I became a prisoner of their preconceived ideas.

I felt trapped and frustrated and found myself wanting to tell them that I had finished five years of college, had my teaching credential, had spent another four years getting my Th.M and was working on my doctorate. I was a teacher like they were—a member of their own profession—but all they could see was the uniform, which limited me to their preconceived ideas about painters. As mentioned earlier, Napoleon stated that a "man becomes the man of his uniform." I discovered that he was right—clothes do make a man. Separated from God, man makes a mad dash for the paint and pillows. The Lord's disciples were no exception.

Royal Robes vs the Servant's Towel

In the last hours of the Lord's life on earth His disciples were involved in a power struggle for the "royal robes" (see Luke 22:24). The disciples thought greatness meant being seen at the right place, at the right time, with the right people. Like us, they needed a graphic description of the robe which *real* people wear. The Lord's living parable recorded in John 13 answered decisively the questions of his friends, and solves the puzzle of your identity and mine. We cannot be beautiful if we are wearing the wrong uniform.

The simple meal in the upper room proved to be one of the most remembered events in human history. John and Peter had labored most of the day over the hot stove preparing and roasting the Passover lamb. One of them had gone to the local supermarket for bread and wine. The table was set with care. The other guests all brought two things to the feast: dirty feet and dirty hearts. They'd probably been to the public baths earlier in the day, but in walking to the site of the upper room had gotten their feet dusty and dirty. Normally a servant was provided at the door to bathe their feet, but no such person was available. No one volunteered because to do so was to admit inferiority and acknowledge the superiority of others.

Christ's actions in becoming a servant to His followers answer the crucial question of our identity. We are servants of the living God! Christ's response illustrates the only posture which produces beauty, and helps us visualize the steps in our own personal pilgrimage to wholeness and beauty.

The first step: *Taking Something Off.* "Jesus knew that the Father had put all things under his power, and that he had come from God and was returning to God, so he got up from the meal, *took off his outer clothing . . .*" (John 13:3-4, NIV, italics added). My wife sometimes teases me about the clothes I wear to work. When I am especially dressed up she often will say, "Seeing some 'heavies' today?" You bet! I feel more confident in certain situations when I am well dressed. The role of servanthood does not demand that I wear shabby clothes, but that my inner attitude and spirit be that of a servant. Christ told His disciples that He was among them "as one who serves." He came to minister and give His life as a ransom. Because His motivation was to serve His friends, He could take off the garments of manhood and stoop to serve.

Philippians 2 provides an interesting comparison to John 13 as it traces Christ's pilgrimage from glory to Gethsemane. Verse six says that Christ, "being in very nature God, did not consider equality with God something to be grasped, but *made himself nothing*, taking the very nature of a servant . . ." (Phil. 2:6-7, NIV, italics added). The disciples wouldn't "take off their outer garments" because they were trying to make themselves *something*. Their hearts were clothed with pride and jealousy and as a result, their hands were unavailable for servant's work. When Christ "laid aside His garments" He served notice to the world that garments of pride, selfishness, insensitivity and indifference to need will not make it in God's divine fashion show. The disciples' refusal to serve one another was ugly.

We are not wired for servanthood. Sin has blown all our circuit breakers and distorted our concept of greatness. Christ's actions teach us that those who line up last wind up first. The way up with God is down. Because we are "wired" to run for the paint and pillows, we cannot become genuine, sincere servants to others until that unhealthy mindset is changed.

Christ's example illustrates the three great realities which make genuine servanthood possible. First, the text reminds us that Jesus was *secure in his authority*. "Jesus knew that the Father had put all things *under his power* . . ." (John 13:3, NIV, italics added). That's what the world wants and doesn't have. Jesus could willingly serve the most selfish, sinful, ungrateful person because He wasn't part of the "power game." His sense of value didn't grow out of His current rating in society's pecking order. Ours shouldn't either. We will continue to perpetuate ugliness as long as we jockey for position in this world's rat race. All authority was given to Christ in heaven and upon earth. You and I are sent out as His ambassador to be mediators of His authority. Imagine that! Sent by the King of the universe to be a part of His purposes. When this great truth finally takes root in our hearts we no longer need to compete, to fight for the "royal robes." A five-hundred-pound gorilla doesn't need to compete. He can sit in the park on the bench of his choice. If God is for you, who can be against you? God *is* for you.

Second, the text reminds us that Christ was *secure in His origin*. "Jesus knew that the Father had put all things under his power, and that *he had come from God . . .*" (John 13:3, NIV, italics added). Jesus, knowing His authority and His origin, arose to serve mankind. Our origin is likewise assured. We have a divine pedigree. Ephesians 1:4 reminds us that God chose us in Christ before the foundation of the world. You had a special place in God's heart before He created the universe. He knew you and loved you before creation itself. What an incredible, liberating truth! How can we question our value? How can we compete? How can we jockey for position? How can we question our uniqueness if God designed each of us as unique individuals before He put the universe together? We must be special! Because we are special, we are set free to serve. Only as I rest in the uniqueness of my sonship, my position in Christ, am I freed to serve without reservation.

Jesus, knowing that the Father had put everything under His control and that He had come from God and was *going to God*, arose from the meal and began to serve His disciples. He alone could serve because He was secure in His position in the scheme of things. He knew His origin and *His destiny*. This third great reality makes genuine servanthood possible for us. He knew His destiny. Without this perspective human life and endeavor is pointless. Without a divine magnetic north pole man finds himself devoid of meaning and purpose. He's adrift on a tour ship with no destination. Christ arose to serve knowing that His past, His present and His future were vitally linked to His Father's purposes. From this base He willingly humbled Himself and served.

We should do no less. Destination glory! We'll see Him face to face and be objects of His love for all eternity. Not one human has ever seen, heard, or come close to conceiving what God is preparing for those that love Him. How can we cling to the paint and pillows, the grave clothes of this world, with a Saviour like that? Chosen by divine love, backed by divine authority, destined for eternal sonship, we are freed to serve. We must therefore willingly strip ourselves of this world's wardrobe of death and "put on the Lord Jesus Christ" (see Rom. 13:14).

A Change of Clothes

The experience of Christ's friend, Lazarus, helps us to visualize the process. Lazarus died and his body was prepared and entombed. That body wasn't going anywhere fast. Jesus came to the grave site and called Lazarus to "come forth." Life immediately flooded through his body, and he sat up and tried to move. Christ brought life, but Lazarus was still a prisoner of his burial garments. Christ divinely commissioned some of Lazarus's friends to go and remove the grave clothes. (See John 11:43, 44.) It should be remembered that Christ could have brought him out of the tomb in a double-knit suit.

Our Lord's decision to let others change Lazarus' clothes leaves us with an interesting analogy. When Christ brings life to us, we still have our grave clothes on. He brings life and then places us into the body of Christ. In this context we are to aid each other in the removal of our "wardrobes of death"—the works of the flesh. As others become God's instruments for healing it is not unusual for Christians to flee for the "paint and pillows." Pastors are particularly adept at this—I should know, I am one. I'm very tempted to write a book titled, *How to Help Your Pastor Join the Body*.

Imagine how ridiculous it would have been for Lazarus to tell his friends, "Bug off! You guys are crazy. Why don't you mind your own business? Your wardrobes don't look so hot, and besides, who gave you the right to judge my garments anyway? After all, I'm on the deacon board, I teach Sunday school, I tithe regularly and I am actively involved in community affairs."

Scripture is clear—we are members of one another. Like it or not, you and I are spiritually interdependent. We are vitally linked together in Christ. The body of Christ is *one body* having many members who are joined to Christ and *to each other*. The hand can't say to the foot, "I have no need of you." We are functionally interdependent and are commanded to mutually edify one another in love. The "one anothers" of the New Testament describe for us something of what that interdependence looks like. To name a few, we are to love, encourage, rebuke, instruct, forgive, and pray for one another, not to mention confessing our faults to one another, and bearing one another's burdens. The body of Christ is not the total provision of God to change our lives, but it is perhaps the most neglected one.

So, what must we take off? Anything which hinders Christ's love for others from being displayed to them through us. In short, what Paul calls the "works of the flesh" in Galatians chapter five. We can fulfill God's purposes for us in the present only if we rest in His choice of us in the past and His plans for us in the future. Sons of God are freed to serve when the great truths about their origin, authority and destiny finally take root in their hearts.

Christ's living parable illustrates a second step in our pilgrimage to beauty. Not only did He take something off, but He "put something on." He girded himself with a towel—the mark of a servant. In so doing He willingly subjected Himself to the needs of others, even though His own needs were acute. Let's face it, the finest towel probably wouldn't win a prize in this world's fashion shows. Most of us aren't fighting for the towel. We want the royal robes. They are the "true" symbols of importance, honor and prestige. Christ didn't agree. He told His friends that the one who would be great must be a servant to all.

God's servants have a distinct wardrobe which is a prerequisite for effective service. The wardrobe is nothing less than Christ Himself! Scripture tells us to "put off" the wardrobe of death and to "put on" Christ (see Col. 3:9; Rom. 13:14). Incredible as it may sound, God's greatest beauty secret is Himself. All believers are partakers of His nature (see II Pet. 1:4) and have become new creatures in Christ (see II Cor. 5:17). Positionally, judicially, full provision for deliverance from the magnetic influence of our ungodly lifestyle has been provided through Christ's substitutionary atonement. Practically, we are continually involved in the process of putting off the old and putting on the new. The key to the process is continually yielding ourselves to Him as instruments for noble purposes. As we walk by means of the Spirit's control, He makes our lives lampstands from which His glory and beauty are displayed.

The last step in our pilgrimage to wholeness and beauty involves *picking something up*. Not only must we "put on Christ," but we must do the *work* of a servant. "After that, he poured water into a basin and began to wash his disciples' feet, drying them with the towel that was wrapped around him" (John 13:5, NIV). Towel wearers and basin bearers—that's what we are. Sons sent to serve, to wash the feet of needy people. This is where the water hits the foot, and it had better not be scalding. As servants we are to bring to needy people that which cleanses and refreshes. We must take the initiative to go to the aid of others, even when our own needs seem overwhelming. Don't forget, Christ had quite a bit on His mind that evening too. The last thing in the world He needed to face was the petty jealousies of His followers. Yet He faced them.

Servants Wanted

Just for the fun of it, let's write a want ad to see if we can get any recruits for servanthood.

Wanted: Men and women who will share their lives with a man named Jesus. He will be a permanent guest, and will expect to be waited upon. Your responsibility will be to see that His every need is met.

1. When He is tired, you will see to it that provisions are made for His rest and relaxation. It will involve washing His feet frequently.

2. When He needs encouragement, you will be sensitive and provide it.

3. When He wants to talk, you will always be available to listen, to share in His joys and sorrows.

4. Should He need food at any hour, regardless of how weary you are, your responsibility is to provide it with a proper spirit.

5. This job will demand that you set aside your life and commit yourself to live for Him.

Fringe Benefits:

1. The satisfaction of His presence.

2. The availability of His resources. He's reputed to be a wealthy man.

3. The prospect of having Him serve you in eternity.

"Be dressed in readiness, and keep your lamps alight. And be like men who are waiting for their master when he returns from the wedding feast, so that they may immediately open the door to him when he comes and knocks. Blessed are those slaves whom the master shall find on the alert when he comes; truly I say to you, that he shall gird himself to serve, and have them recline at table, and will come up and wait on them. . . . Be ready; for the Son of Man is coming at an hour that you do not expect" (Luke 12:35-40, NASB).

Does that sound good? I know what you're thinking. "Aldrich, if Christ were available to serve, we'd all do it. There's a vast difference between Christ and my husband. Any resemblance is purely accidental. Living with him makes walking on water look easy." Friend, Christ is available. He said, "He who receives whomever I send receives Me; and he who receives Me receives Him who sent Me" (John 13:20, NASB). Wow! That's powerful. *A servant is someone who receives whomever Christ sends.* And the person who receives the sent one receives the sender.

Matthew 25 records an interesting illustration of Christ's coming to us in the lives of others. Although the primary application of this passage is the future tribulation period, it's description of true servanthood complements Christ's statement in John 13. The scenario Matthew describes is a future judgment which takes place after Christ's second coming. The people on Christ's right receive an invitation to join Him in His Father's kingdom. Those on the left hear Christ say, "Depart from me, you who are cursed, into the eternal fire prepared for the devil and his angels" (Matt. 25:41, NIV). Christ explains that those who were invited to share in His kingdom fed Him when He was hungry, gave Him drink when He was thirsty, visited Him when He was a stranger, clothed Him, tended Him when He was sick and visited Him in prison. Those on His right are dumbfounded by His statement. They ask, "Lord, when did we see you hungry and feed you, or thirsty and give you something to drink? When did we see you a stranger and invite you in, or needing clothes and clothe you? When did we see you sick or in prison and go to visit you?" (Matt. 25:37-39, NIV). Christ answers, "I tell you the truth, whatever you did for one of the least of these brothers of mine, you did for me" (v. 40, NIV). The condemned on his left ask the same questions, and the Lord replies, "Whatever you did not do for one of the least of these, you did not do for me" (v. 45, NIV).

A servant is one who receives whomever Christ sends. The true servant recognizes every encounter as an opportunity to love another for Christ's sake. So who has the Lord sent to you? Your husband, wife, brother, sister, mother, dad, friend, classmate, employee? Are you in competition with these "sent ones" because of uncertainty concerning your origin, authority and destiny? A chosen son sent to serve—there is no higher calling.

In one of his essays Charles Lamb describes a quaint old couple who puzzled and amused their friends. Although they were poverty stricken they always carried themselves with a courtly dignity as though they were great people. There was a reason for their courtly bearing—they had a noble ancestor. That fact cast a glamor over their lives and helped them cope with life's adversities. We may be poor, frightened, sinful, foolish and ignorant, but we should bear ourselves with dignity and beauty because we have a noble ancestor—we are children of God.

Humpty-Dumpty was pushed, and the king's best men couldn't put him back together again. Sin has broken all of us, and we can't put ourselves back together, but God can.

Chapter 6

A BALANCED DIET
SOUL FOOD

Crawdads always intrigued me. I used to stop off at the crawdad hole on the way home from school and lose all sense of time. I guess they were exciting to observe and catch because they were fast, and they could pinch pretty hard. The combination of speed, risk and challenge proved to be irresistible. I learned a lot about their habits through trial and error.

After I graduated from grade school, we didn't cross paths again until my college days when once again I was called upon to study crawdads. One experiment has always stood out in my mind. With apologies to any science buffs, I'll try to remember what happened.

The crawdad has a most intriguing balance mechanism. He has two tiny receptacles in his head which he keeps filled with grains of sand. As he moves through the water, the grains of sand move in response to his position, and their movement is transmitted to his brain by tiny cilia which detect the shifting and moving of the grains of sand. Our task was to remove the sand and replace it with metal filings. Having done this we would place a magnet near the crawdad, and by so doing completely disorient him. We could get him swimming upside down and sideways by use of the magnet. Normally the law of gravity kept him properly aligned with his environment. When we introduced metal filings and a magnet into his life, we were able to supersede the law of gravity with the law of magnetism, and totally disorient him.

Life is a lot like that. We make a noble effort to keep ourselves aligned with truth and yet are very susceptible to "metal filings and magnets," which can disorient us. There are those who believe, for example, that Paul wrote the King James Bible. Others believe that Sunday School is as old as the New Testament Church and therefore a New Testament imperative. Many believe that the pastor is to do the work of the ministry. Many pastors believe that they are *the* minister, the administrator, the ruler.

Thousands believe that Christians don't do this and don't do that. Many believe that the Bible teaches that we should pass an offering plate every Sunday, and that the idea of an altar call comes straight from the pen of Paul. Many believe that musical instruments should be banned from the church. The church I grew up in has a specific rule forbidding the playing of a guitar in the "sanctuary."

I'm not making a value judgment about any of these beliefs, except to say that most of them are culturally determined. Why do we meet at mid-morning on Sunday for our church services? Because in agrarian America the farmer couldn't get his cows milked and his chores done any earlier. Is there anything wrong with mid-morning church? Absolutely not, as long as we don't believe it is a biblical mandate. The Bible gives man freedom to assemble and worship on any day of the week, at any time.

Unfortunately, there are some commonly held "truths" which can be harmful and can hinder our expression of God's glorious nature. The health food movement has done us a favor by reminding us that "we are what we eat." A truly beautiful person is a healthy person, and a

70

healthy person is one who eats properly. Likewise, a healthy soul is one fed a proper diet of wholesome truth. Bad "soul food" sooner or later reflects itself in the body, no matter how well pampered it is. Youth can cover a sick soul with a healthy body for awhile, but ugliness is compounded with age if the soul is neglected. Some of the most beautiful people have wrinkles, crowsfeet, bulges and sags. The older we grow, the more important inner beauty becomes, because God's glory is more clearly seen in weakness.

Beauty demands a balanced diet of "soul food." The church, the body of Christ, is designed as a "divine cafeteria" and as such is a major source of the Christian's spiritual nourishment. If this is true, why are so many Christians suffering from spiritual malnutrition? The answer is simple: they are not getting a balanced diet. Acts chapter two teaches us that the Holy Spirit builds beautiful bodies four ways, by ministering to the *whole* man. Let's look at these four parts of a balanced diet.

A Balanced Spiritual Diet

First, the Holy Spirit builds strong bodies by leading us into vital learning experiences. Acts 2:42 reminds us that the believers in the early church were "continually devoting themselves to the apostles' teaching (NASB). The church is responsible to provide the believer with a basic knowledge of the Word. There are facts to be learned, information to be mastered. The Bible is propositional, and its propositions are weapons which are designed to assault the fortresses of untruth in our minds and take captive every thought in obedience to Christ.

But Christianity is not just an "intellectual" trip. My goal is not just to fill my frontal lobe with facts. Impression minus expression leads to spiritual depression. Our

71

churches are full of people who "sit, soak and sour." Hearing a sermon once or twice a week is not enough. No matter how gifted the pastor, sitting and listening to him alone is not a balanced diet. We are to love God with the total person, not just the mind. Some, for example, love God with the strength of mind and the weakness of the emotions. This produces the stuffy theologian, the self-appointed expert on trivia. I have observed an interesting phenomenon with new Christians. In the first few months of their Christian pilgrimage they have an insatiable desire for information. They sit in the front row and hang on the pastor's every word. They take notes, they ask questions, they joy in their new discoveries. But something inevitably happens at about the one year mark. They suddenly wake up and realize that there must be something more.

And there is. Luke reminds us that the Holy Spirit also builds beautiful bodies *by leading us into vital fellowship experiences.* This is the second element in a balanced diet.

Fellowship is not sharing coffee and doughnuts at the conclusion of the sermon. It implies sharing and exchanging something. It is the deep spiritual community in Christ which believers share when they gather together as Christ's bride.

Unfortunately, most of our social involvements have very little fellowship. We come together like marbles, and ricochet around the room. Our masks are firmly fixed, designed to complement our paint and pillows. Often we long to reach out to touch and be touched, to intersect another life at a deep level, but the risk is too great. The others look so adequate, so happy, so contented, so self-sufficient. The church today suffers from a fellowship crisis. It is neither experiencing nor demonstrating that "fellowship of the Holy Spirit" (II Cor. 13:14) that characterized the New Testament Church.

Yet fellowship is absolutely essential because it is the context in which the giftedness of the body is made available to help me at my point of need. It is men coming together like grapes, crushed, with skins of ego broken. Their broken lives mingle together like the new wine of crushed grapes, and they discover something of what it means to be members of one another. The most significant, life-changing learning takes place in this social interaction. As hard as that truth is on the pastor's ego, it is true. If the data of the behavioral sciences didn't clearly demonstrate its truth, our Lord's ministry certainly would. He was under little compulsion to "cover material." He marked men for a lifetime by being with them, eating with them, using the challenges and problems of everyday living as an opportunity to learn. His disciples learned the principles of interdependence and the mutuality of ministry. Christ's motivation was not to "fill jugs," but to light lamps. This second dimension of a balanced diet means that every Christian needs to be part of a "small band of men" with which he can share his life. The church must make provision for its members to be significantly involved in the giftedness of the total body.

I sometimes hear people say, "But I want some 'deep' teaching, and I won't get it in a small group." In most cases such comments show a lack of understanding of the way in which change takes place in human lives. God has three major inputs into our lives which the Holy Spirit uses to change our value systems. The first is the *written word*. This is the road map, the intellectual framework, the propositional statement of the Christian faith. Second, is the *incarnate Word*, Christ himself, whose presence in the life through the Spirit is a source of strength, comfort and instruction. Third, the *"lived out word,"* the Christian whose life is a visual aid of truth. Christians are not only to "know truth," but to "be truth." To "be truth" is to "be beautiful," because truth is the basis of beauty. Paul tells us that we are "living epistles," read by all men (see II Cor. 3:2, 3). This tells me that if I need wisdom, God not only supplies it from the "inspired epistles," but also through "living epistles."

In II Corinthians 7:6 we see how God works directly through His people to minister to other believers. In that passage Paul tells us that God comforted him by the coming of Titus. Titus became a direct channel, the means by which Paul experienced *God's comfort*. How do you know God loves you? Certainly because of the cross, but also because you have experienced His love through other believers. It is important that we visualize the resources of God flowing through all three of these channels or we are apt to shut ourselves off from much of what God has provided for us. It is not enough to simply "continue in the apostles' doctrine."

Our values are basically socially anchored. This means that we tend to associate with people who represent and support the values and beliefs which we feel are important. The new Christian who does not develop a new web of relationships within the Christian community will find growth much more difficult because his old associations will probably not model and reinforce the Christian value system. Paul's letter to the church at Thessalonica provides amazing insights into the social dimensions of behavioral change. Paul reminds the believers of the *life* he lived among them for their sake. Next, he says, "You also became imitators of us . . ." (I Thess. 1:6). He does not say, "You became disciples of our theological system," although I'm sure they did. Paul is saying, "Our lives became models for your lives, and you became imitators of us." Through "fellowship" (the fusion of their lives, values, dreams and aspirations) a transformation took place: they became like Paul the man. There is no imitation without intimacy. In the second chapter Paul reminds them that he not only imported the gospel to them, but also his *very life* because the people at Thessalonica had become very dear to him. We emulate those that we esteem. We copy those who challenge us, we imitate those who represent a God-like life. Paul told his followers to become imitators of him.

This tendency to emulate is especially visible in children. I spent eight summers counseling at Trout Creek Camp near Portland, Oregon. It was fun to observe the "modeling concept" in action. If your fourth grade boys thought you were really great, it wasn't long until they started to copy your mannerisms. If I walked around with my hands in my back pocket, or used a particular expression regularly, soon most of my campers were doing the same thing. Even we adults try to be like those we respect. It always amused me at seminary to observe some of the budding "preachers" turning out with the same gestures and mannerisms as their instructors. But the process doesn't stop with imitation. Those who imitate become models. In I Thessalonians 1:7 Paul points out that those who imitated him became models for all the churches in Macedonia.

They experienced a relationship which changed them, and they in turn became models which influenced the churches all over Asia Minor. This illustration teaches us that there is *little transformation without transfusion*. Our Lord illustrates this change mechanism in Luke 6:40 where He says that the pupil who is fully taught will be like his teacher. Notice that it doesn't say he will *know what his teacher knows*.

Let's bring this principle down to earth. Isn't the most frustrating thing about your children the fact that they are becoming just like you? Have you ever noticed that the weaknesses which irritate you most in your children are *your* weaknesses? I wonder where they got them. Children have a tremendous capacity to close their ears to advice and open their eyes to example. So do you.

The body of Christ is a transforming community, a divinely gifted group of believers who become agents of healing when fellowship is a vital part of their lifestyle. Sunday morning normally exposes the body to the limited giftedness of one man.

The Valve of a Small Group

A small group provides an opportunity for the giftedness of the body to become available to individual needs. Unfortunately not every small group maximizes these opportunities. Often they are just as stilted and formal as the morning service. Let me suggest three things that should happen in an effective support group. First, the members should gather to share the *word* together. Bible study is central to effective fellowship. This can involve the study of a particular text or the sharing of the results of personal Bible study during the week. This provides a framework for prayer and worship.

Second, the members should share their *schedules*, the important events, appointments and meetings of their week. Many times I've heard men say how much it meant to them to have a member of their supportive group call and pray with them over the phone about a crucial event on their calendar. Sharing of schedule serves as a reminder that our vocation is our mission field and helps us see people in a new light.

Third, we need to share our *relationships* together. This means that I share how I'm doing in my relationship to God, how I'm doing in my marriage, how my children are progressing, and any concerns which I have about those relationships. Such sharing of life and growth is not new.

Back in the mid 1700's John Wesley placed thousands of his converts in small groups for growth and nurture. These people agreed that they would meet together once a week to reveal the true state of their souls to each other, sharing plainly the faults they had committed in thought, word, and deed.

They were not admitted to the fellowship bands until

they were willing for the members of the fellowship to search their hearts "to the bottom," sharing whatever they thought and felt, and whatever they had heard. The members agreed to share everything in their hearts, "without exception, without disguise and without reserve." Wesley believed in the individual priesthood of the believer! He felt that every Christian should be and feel responsible for every other believer. In a word, He believed in accountability. So they shared the Word and their schedules and relationships, and encouraged growth through accountability.

We need to stimulate each other to love and good works by holding each other accountable. To know and not to do is not to know at all. When I speak at conferences I get so absorbed in the process I tend to neglect my wife. I shared this with my supportive fellowship, and they got me to commit at least two hours each day to my wife at the next conference. I agreed. At least three times during the week of that conference in Colorado I got long distance calls from Newport Beach, California to see if I was following through. These men love me. How do I know? Because they care enough to be catalysts in my life, whatever the cost.

Accountability means that I am held responsible for who I am and what I do. It is something I give to others as a sacred trust. When it is all boiled down it is simply love in action as others enable me to grow towards wholeness by checking in on various areas of my life. Accountability is the Body of Christ in action, seeking to fight infection and bring about healing and health.

The Holy Spirit builds strong bodies a third way: *By leading us into vital worship experiences.* Acts 2:42 records that the believers continued to pray and break bread together daily. Worship is acknowledging the presence of an infinite God and responding with praise, thanksgiving and obedience. The proclamation of the Word plus the shared experiences of God's faithfulness prepare us for worship. It can occur anywhere and any time. Sometimes it happens on Sunday morning. Worship is one of the greatest healing forces in the body of Christ. We either worship or worry, it's as simple as that. Worrying people are not worshiping people. When we are caught up with the greatness of God we don't ask for the pennies in His hand because we have His hand. When we have His hand, we don't need answers because He is the answer. Beautiful people learn, share and worship together.

A fourth element in a balanced diet is that the Holy Spirit builds beautiful people by leading us into *vital service opportunities.*

The United States military forces are training men to fight so that they will never have to fight. We believe that if we keep our forces strong they will never be needed. So do many churches. Vast numbers of Christians would rather go to church than be the church. The church is not a building, it is people in relationship. Yet some view the church as a local department store. They all come to the "store" in the morning, and once the "saints" are safely inside, they lock the doors and start selling goods to each other.

The song is right. There is joy in serving Jesus. As we give, we get. As we bless, we are blessed. As we give beauty, we become beautiful. We are gifted by God to serve His purposes, and our fulfillment in life is directly linked to our utilization of our gifts, abilities and resources, to accomplish them.

I attended a management training seminar recently in which the speaker said that poor people ought to take rich people out to dinner. What he was really saying is that success leaves clues. So does beauty. Beautiful people have a clean inner landscape and eat a balanced diet. How's your "soul food"? Have you been eating a balanced diet at the King's table? His menu involves a balance between doctrine, fellowship, worship and service.

Chapter 7

BEAUTIFYING THE BEAUTY PARLOR

An ancient manuscript compared the church to Noah's Ark. It said "If it were not for the storm on the outside, we couldn't stand the stench on the inside." To put it bluntly, the writer was talking about spiritual "body odor." The divine beauty parlor stinks. Can a man put fire in his bosom and not be burned? Can I be an active part of a local body which is diseased and remain healthy? Can I be a light if members of my church family ice skate down the aisles as God's frozen people?

The beauty of God's redemptive love is *declared* in Scripture, is *demonstrated* at the cross, and is to be *displayed* in the body. God has designed the local church family as the primary context in which the possession of His nature surfaces and becomes an observable, tangible phenomenon. The church is not only the display case for His love, it is the *beauty parlor*. But it cannot display what it does not possess. It cannot illustrate God's unity if it is marked by divisiveness. It cannot illustrate faithfulness and truth if its people are feuding and gossiping. Ideally, the wider our exposure to the giftedness of the body, the greater our potential for beauty.

The problem confronting many church families, many "beauty parlors," is one of definition. The Pharisees thought they were beautiful, and paraded around like proud peacocks. They reinforced each other's perceptions because they valued the same things, and pursued the same goals.

People can adjust to almost anything, including stench. Sometimes the stench itself becomes the most highly prized commodity. The Lord warned against some of the "stench" which could creep into the beauty parlor in His parables recorded in Matthew 13. A good description of ugliness helps us pursue beauty. Every believer should be a guardian of the beauty parlor, because his beauty is directly related to its beauty. Our values and ideals are socially anchored. To be beautiful we need to associate with beauty.

In Matthew 13 our Lord uses parables to provide a prophetic picture of the condition of the beauty parlor during the present church age. The parable of the sower and four soils teaches that the gospel will be preached, and there will be a mixed response ranging from indifference to full acceptance. The second parable also involves the symbols of a sower and seed, except that the seed is not a message, but *men*. God takes those who respond to the gospel (the first seed) and they *become* seed. Jesus calls them "good" seed. The word "good" is *kalos*, a Greek word for beauty. Here we observe that God sows two kinds of seed: a blessed message and a beautiful man.

Bear in mind that a man devoid of relationships has little potential for revealing his character. I may be a giving, loving, moral being, but if I live as a hermit what I am is not apparent. It becomes apparent as soon as life impinges upon me in such a way that I must respond to another person or to events involving another person as a spectator. The test of beauty is response. The test of maturity is not knowledge but relationship. Good seeds are people who exhibit God-like responses in a hell-like world, who respond to ugliness with beauty, who exhibit beauty by acknowledging their own digressions into ugliness. The beauty of the good seed is God, who is expressed in relationships. The healthier the relationships, the greater the beauty.

A Little Leaven

Another parable of Jesus helps us see some of the most dangerous diseases of the body. "He spoke another parable unto them; 'The kingdom of heaven is like leaven, which a woman took, and hid in three pecks of meal, until it was all leavened'" (Matt. 13:33, NASB).

The Jewish listeners would immediately associate leaven with the events of the Passover. The Israelites had lived in Egypt for over 400 years. During this time they had passed on leaven "starters" from household to household, from father to son to grandson. When God finally delivered them from Egypt he told them to leave their yeast behind. They were to cut all their ties with Egypt and its old way of life. They were told to take unleavened bread as a symbol of the purity of a new beginning. The ancients saw leaven (yeast) as a symbol of corruption. Plutarch said that yeast is the "offspring of corruption, and corrupts the mass of dough with which it is mixed." Rabbinical writers regularly used leaven as a symbol of evil. As we will observe, Paul and Christ also use it as a symbol for that which is evil. The point of the parable seems to be that the woman shouldn't have put the leaven into the dough.

One of the key interpretive questions is what the three measures of meal symbolize. Abraham had Sarah prepare three measures of meal when the angelic beings fellowshipped with him (Gen. 18:6); Gideon offered unleavened bread to the angelic visitors who called on him (Judg. 6:19-20). The grain offering was to be offered without leaven to God, and what remained was to be eaten by Aaron and his sons (Lev. 6:14-18). Flour, the product of grain which has been crushed, is a beautiful symbol of the New Testament concept of fellowship or *koinonia*. It speaks of individual kernels broken and crushed together to make something that is palatable and attractive. In the parable our Lord suggests that something (leaven) will be introduced into the body of Christ which will hinder the fellowship of the body and consequently harm its beauty and its effectiveness as a beauty parlor. In parable form, the Lord looks down through the course of history and sees threats to the fellowship of His people.

In Matthew 16:6, the only other time our Lord refers to leaven, He warns His disciples against the deadly leavens (the teachings) of the Pharisees and Sadducees. How appropriate! The disciples were the future leaders of the church, and guardians of its life. The Lord warns them against allowing the teachings of the Pharisees to influence the life of the church.

The Leaven of Hypocrisy

The leaven of the Pharisees is religious externalism or hypocrisy. It's ritual without reality, form without function, motions without meaning. When hypocrisy is the lifestyle of the church, significant relationships become nearly impossible to cultivate. This is true because the lifestyle of the hypocrite is the lifestyle of the fugitive. It encourages people to parade "perfection" rather than "progress," in spite of the specific admonitions to let our *progress* be made known to all men.

The Greek actor was called a "hypocrite" because he "spoke from under a mask." We cannot afford that luxury, because the "mask" mentality encourages us to remain in protracted infancy. God calls us to speak the truth in love, so that we may grow up in all respects unto Christ (see Eph.

4:15). Love without truth is mushy sentimentality. Truth without love is brutality.

Hypocrisy expresses itself in many ways. Here are a few symptoms: 1) A judgmental, critical attitude towards others. 2) An attempt to be something which I know I am not. 3) A lifestyle in which I cover and hide rather than share my life with others. 4) A false piety based on self-determined standards which make me look good. 5) Judging others on external appearance. 6) Self-righteous, self-justifying attitudes in which I refuse to accept responsibility for my errors or neglects.

The Leaven of Rationalism

The second leaven is *rationalism*. The Sadducees were anti-supernaturalists in that they didn't believe in the resurrection or angelic beings. In a religious context, rationalism is limiting God to my finite, inadequate capabilities. It is professing a belief in an almighty God and living totally in a humanistic framework. The term describes a people who have lost their vision of the sovereignty of God and are incapable of believing in God-sized goals. Put quite simply, rationalism is unbelief. Our Lord warns against allowing it to permeate our fellowship like leaven. It siphons away the supernatural dimensions of life and reduces Christianity to nothing but a glorified humanism. Churches afflicted with this malady are continually taking their pulse and declaring "It cannot be done." The non-Christian sees little difference between such churches and the local library committee. Unbelief is deadly because it produces pessimism and negative thinking.

Rationalism expresses itself in many ways. Here are some of its symptoms: 1) Rationalizing inadequacy rather than believing God wills its removal. 2) Believing that I alone am the captain of my fate, and no one can help solve my problems. I must do it myself. 3) A "we tried that once" attitude. 4) A worship of form and tradition. 5) An unwillingness to risk myself to fulfill God's purposes. 6) A strong desire to "save face" at all costs. 7) A practical unbelief of the promises of God. 8) A non-existent prayer life.

The Leaven of Impurity

Paul introduces a third deadly leaven in I Corinthians 5. It is the leaven of *impurity*. The Pharisee attempts to appear pure, while the rationalist redefines purity to include his impurity. If the body is to produce beauty, it must not harbor ugliness. We must separate from the unclean *brother* who refuses to respond to God's call to a life of purity.

Each fall at "Aldrich Acres" we boys had to pick apples. Box after box was stored away for winter in the vegetable and fruit shed. From these boxes of apples would come glorious apple pies, hot applesauce topped off with ice-cream, and gallons of cider. But the price of such goodies was constant vigilance. We had to sort through the boxes and bins on a regular basis because one unattended rotten apple soon spread its corruption to its nearest neighbors. Impurity spreads in the same way if it is not checked. Love and impurity cannot exist together. As a result the believer is to separate himself from the leaven of impurity.

Separation is not isolation from the world, it is separation from anyone who habitually contaminates the purity of the body. As suggested earlier, no clever arrangement of rotten eggs will make a good omelet.

Are you part of the problem or part of the solution? Love springs from a pure heart. So does beauty.

The Leaven of Legalism

A last leaven is found in Galatians chapter five. It is the *leaven of legalism*. Legalism is perhaps the greatest enemy of beauty and grace; and our churches are full of it. Legalism, like a frontal lobotomy, cuts the nerve of creativity, vitality and beauty and leaves its victims alive but not living, breathing but not beautiful. We are all legalists by nature. It seems so much easier to draw up lists and bury ourselves behind self-imposed limits than to understand our freedom in Christ. The legalist is a prisoner of other people's expectations. He usually has little impact upon the non-Christian world because he creates many artificial and unbiblical "barriers." He excuses his lack of effectiveness by blaming it on the "apostasy" or the "last days."

Here are a few symptoms of the leaven of legalism: 1) A decided preference for the old wineskins. Anything new is considered liberal. 2) An attitude of suspicion towards anyone who disagrees with his prescribed lifestyle. 3) Guilt by association. The one who mixes regularly with non-Christians is often viewed as compromising his Christianity. 4) A strong need for uniformity. All Christians must eat, drink, think and believe the same. 5) Views the non-Christian as the enemy rather than the victim of the enemy. 6) Judges the spiritual life of the Christian on the basis of the things he doesn't do. He generally has a negative focus. 7) Often has difficulty developing significant relationships because his attitude of legalism makes intimacy difficult. 8) A tendency to major on the minors. 9) An appeal to the letter of the law rather than the spirit of it.

If beauty is to become a way of life, we must take beauty seriously. The beauty parlor must produce beauty. To do so means to face ugliness with integrity. To be beautiful, we need to associate with beautiful people. Beautiful people are transparent, open, sharing, giving people. They are people of faith and hope. God is alive and well in their midst, and they acknowledge His presence with thanksgiving and praise. Beautiful people take purity and holiness seriously, and are making progress in that direction. Their lives are creative and vital because they have been freed from the bondage of the "old wineskins" and have entered into the abundant life which Christ promises to provide. Beauty is caught, not taught.

If the beauty parlor isn't beautiful, perhaps God can use you as an instrument to move it towards beauty. Commit yourself to two or three others and become a source of beauty. Eliminate the leavens. Bury them and refuse to allow their ugly heads to rear themselves. Be prepared for an invasion. Beauty is contagious. If some of your Christian associates are suffering from a severe case of "hardening of the categories" it might be well to pray for Christian friends who are filled with the love of Christ, and make them the change agents in your life. You need the beauty parlor, and it needs you. Your membership in a loving, caring supportive family where the gifts of the Spirit are free to shape and mold your life is a key to your beauty.

Chapter 8

BASICS OF
A BEAUTIFUL
MARRIAGE

One of the most clever Volkswagen ads shows an impeccable little car—with a flat tire. The caption reads, "Nobody's Perfect."

When two imperfect people fall in love, strange things happen. Logic and rationality go out the window. Blindness sets in. Overcome with ecstatic paralysis, they float away on their cloud built for two.

Marriage, however, has a way of ending this glowing period of simulated perfection. Where two or more are gathered together, someone is going to have a flat tire. It doesn't take long for the newlyweds to discover that "everything in one person nobody's got." They soon learn that a marriage license is just a learner's permit, and ask with agony, "Is there life after marriage?"

An old Arab proverb states that marriage begins with a prince kissing an angel and ends with a bald-headed man looking across the table at a fat lady. Socrates told his students, "By all means marry. If you get a good wife, twice blessed you will be. If you get a bad wife, you'll become a philosopher." Count Herman Keyserling said it well when he stated that "The essential difficulties of life do not end, but rather begin with marriage."

In California's Orange County, where I live, almost half of the marriages are ending in divorce. Something in our modern day of wash and wear wedding dresses has gone wrong. You probably heard of the bride who doubled the wedding cake recipe and froze one. Let's face it. Husbands and wives who really love each other have become an endangered species. Divorce is up 800% in the last 100 years.

Someone has said that marriage is like a violin. Once the beautiful music is over, the strings are still attached. But what if the blossoms haven't all fallen off the marital tree? Suppose the fat lady loves her bald-headed husband much more than during courtship, and he still thinks she is wonderful? Then, friend, you have seen a miracle.

Every relationship moves automatically towards separation and concealment. Marriage is potentially the most intimate human relationship and as a result has the greatest potential for good or evil, for beauty or ugliness. We want all our relationships, especially marriage, to be centers of beauty, the keyboard from which the beauty of God sounds forth for all to hear. But such a lofty goal is neither easy nor automatic. God is the designer of marriage and only He can make it work. Marriages don't fail, people fail, and people fail because they live their lives without God. A marriage without Christ has the potential for togetherness, but never oneness, because oneness is a spiritual, divine quality. The shared life of God is the secret of beauty in marriage.

In this chapter we will focus on love and marriage in the beginning, and see that from the beginning of human history we were destined to be bearers of God's beauty. The institution of marriage itself is designed to be a relationship in which the nature of God is displayed.

It should be pointed out that the Bible is not a marriage manual in the strictest sense, and makes no such claims for itself. Human relationships are vital and dynamic, not static or mechanical, and as a result their functioning cannot be governed by mere check lists or rules. In the Scriptures we see principles which the Holy Spirit uses to help men and women make proper adjustments in their unique marriage relationships which enable them to produce beauty.

Insights from Creation

The creation account provides some remarkable insights which are foundational in developing a lifestyle of beauty.

First, *man is more than the divine union of the material elements of this earth.* Genesis 2:7-8 reveals that God took the elements of the earth and formed man's body, and into this body He breathed the breath of life.

This creative act tells us that man is not an isolated unity. His nature is not self-enclosed. He is more than a material being. He cannot be comprehended by looking at man alone. Unlike the animal world, man is the fusion of earthly dust and divine breath. He is the product of the blending of the material and immaterial worlds. To see man apart from God is not to see man. Man's relationship to God is not a crutch, it is not something added to his nature, it is an essential part of his nature. Do you get the message? If God is not part of your life, you're not normal. As Pascal said, you've got a God-shaped vacuum in your heart which can only be filled by God the creator made known through Jesus Christ. God is the fuel of the human spirit, and without Him our lives and relationships ping, miss and knock.

Second, *man is an image bearer of God.*

When we talk about the image of God in man, we are not simply saying that man, like God, has attributes like God's attributes, although in some measure he does. We are

89

pointing instead, to a living, dynamic, essential relationship between God and man which makes man truly man.

The fact that man is an image bearer of God suggests a *purpose* for man and also a *quality* of life. As an image bearer of an infinite God he possesses such great potential that the only adequate center for his life is God.

Third, *man is more than man plus God*. Man, like the Trinity, is a being-in-relationship. Consequently, man plus God does not equal "man." Adam had a relationship with God, and yet God said, "It is not good for the man to be alone" (Gen. 2:18, NASB). Woman plus God does not equal "man." Genesis 5:2 tells us that God "created them male and female, and He blessed them and named *them* [man and woman] Man" (NASB, italics added).

"Man" consists of two distinct personal components. "Man" is male and female. God said that the two "shall become one flesh" (Gen. 2:24, NASB). The blending of two into one flesh most accurately reflects God's nature. He created them (male and female) in His image. His image, His attributes, His essential being, then, are most accurately reflected in the "oneness" created by the joining of male and female.

God drove Adam's incompleteness home to him in a unique way. God told him to name the animals. Two fat looking beasts waddle towards him and he says, "You look like hippos. I'm going to name you Mr. and Mrs. Joe Hippo." And they walk off into the sunset with love in their eyes. Two skyscraper-like creatures walk towards him. "You look like giraffes. I'm naming you Mr. and Mrs. George Giraffe." And they walk off into the sunset with their necks entwined and with love in their eyes. Two prickly looking balls of fur walk towards him, and he steps back and says, "You're to be called Mr. and Mrs. Porcupine." And he watches them amble away, paw in paw into the sunset.

The sun sets and Adam has his seven minutes with God, but even fellowship with his creator doesn't fill up his empty places. He is lonely. His problem is not a geographical loneliness, not isolation in space. Nor is it a vocational problem. There are no "No Help Wanted" signs in Eden. It is a constitutional problem. It is the condition of being less than a complete person. Adam's creation was not complete without Eve. Man is not man without woman. There is an interdependence between man and woman whether married or unmarried. Male and female are two complementary halves who join together to make a new whole. Each becomes the center and source for the other. Man's deficiency was not solved by providing him with another male companion.

Adam needed more than society. He needed someone who would be his perfect counterpart, a complement, one who would "fill up his empty places." Eve's primary role was to be God's instrument to help bring Adam to his fullest potential as a man. Ephesians 5 shows that man's love for his wife is designed to provide a context in which she can grow and reveal her beauty and uniqueness (see vv. 25-33).

It's very important to observe at this point that maleness and femaleness are not just physical properties. With the joining together of male and female in holy matrimony, the image of God is complete. Before the creation of woman, man's masculinity, his sexuality had no meaning. Woman gave his sexuality meaning and significance. She was God's special gift to man, the noblest creation God could conceive for His highest creature. This is one reason she is to be revered and honored. She is God's provision for the incompleteness of man.

Fourth, *human sexuality is a God-given capacity for relationship*. God did not create male and female as arbitrary categories so they could be fruitful and replenish the earth. Rather, he made them different in gender. As such, they find fulfillment through a relationship to their creator and through marriage. God ordained marriage as the context in which the sexuality, the full maleness and femaleness of the partners, can be fully realized. Marriage is based on bodies. Bodies are in. In fact, some of my best friends have bodies.

But if physical union in marriage is simply the joining of bodies, it is far less than God purposed it to be. It takes much more than glands and a central nervous system to make love. A purely physical relationship is less than personal, and as a result not really sexual in the biblical sense. If there is no communion of hearts, minds and wills, the relationship is neither personal or sexual.

If a marriage is the primary context for revealing God's beauty, then the most private, intimate moments in the relationship must be beautiful and sacred. Marriage may be based on bodies, but sex is not what you do, it is what you are. It is a function of the total person. The enjoyment of the physical union is based on the harmony of soul and spirit which exists between husband and wife and God. This harmony or unity is God's wedding gift he delights to give to those who respond to His grace. Apart from God there can be no wholeness, no blending of personality and, hence, no real beauty. Sin has corrupted the divine image of God in man and broken man's relationship with God. Without a renewed relationship to God there can be no union of two persons in their sexual totality. Sexuality can only be completed and fulfilled by those who are experiencing God renewing His image in their lives. In a very real sense, beauty is tested in the bedroom. If I bring to that relationship the beauty of a pure heart, a clear conscience and a transparent life, it becomes sacred communion. If the spirit of the marriage is healthy, it will be evidenced in the physical relationship. God's work in me allows me to bring to my wife a richness and fulness which would be impossible apart from His grace. The model of His unconditional love for me helps me love my wife. His forgiveness of me helps me forgive. My security in Him helps me provide security.

Sexuality is a God-given capacity for relationship. It must never be used as a weapon to manipulate or control. It provides a spiritual, emotional, physical intimacy which blends two beings into a blessed oneness only when it is motivated by a harmony of soul and spirit which God alone makes possible.

Fifth, *the blending of male and female sexuality provides the most effective context for displaying God's beauty.* Notice I did not say the only context.

Being made in the image of God means that man is created to reveal the glory of God in human relationships. Central to the concept of the "image of God" is the idea of "making visible." We are called lights, and we function as such when the beauty of God's character is reflected through the relationships we sustain. One of man's responsibilities is to be a representative of God through being His image on earth. Everyone who serves as a channel, as a reflector of God's light, is fulfilling his responsibility and destiny as an image bearer.

He is called a light, not because he originates it, but because he reflects it. The fruit, or evidence, of the light of God is goodness, righteousness and truth according to Ephesians 5:9. Romans 8:29 says that the believer's destiny is to be conformed to the image of God's Son. We are to be like Him, the one who perfectly reflects the glory of God and bears the very stamp of the Father's nature (see Heb. 1:3).

The marriage relationship is the most intimate and difficult relationship which a human sustains. The true reflector, the light, the effective image bearer of God is one who demonstrates goodness, righteousness and truth in *that* relationship, as well as the other relationships of life. All believers, single or married, are image bearers. If we love each other, the world knows we are disciples of Christ. The greatest miracle, however, is a husband loving his wife as Christ loves you and me, and a wife willingly accepting the leadership of her husband. That's beauty.

Up to this point we've been discussing the *potential* for beauty which exists in being an image bearer of God Himself. His Spirit produces beautiful fruit as we respond in obedience to Him. This fruit is evidenced by the manner in which we respond to people, events and circumstances. Our goal is God-like responses in every relationship, especially marriage.

Principles for Beauty

The creation account also provides us with some *principles* which make our potential for beauty a real possibility. Principle number one: *cut the umbilical cord to your parents.* "For this cause [marriage] a man shall leave his father and his mother . . ." (Gen. 2:24, NASB). An old proverb says that "No home is big enough for two families."

A marriage, like a newborn infant, cannot grow unless the umbilical cord is cut. Often well-meaning parents are at the heart of the newlyweds' earliest and most painful disharmony. In-laws often become outlaws, robbing the new relationship of its beauty and love. Many can identify with the man who responded to a knock on his front door. Upon opening it he was confronted by a lady who asked, "Will you donate something to the Old Ladies' Home?" Without hesitation he replied, "With pleasure. Help yourself to my mother-in-law." There can be no "cleaving" without leaving.

A lifestyle prepackaged by parents is doomed to fail. The husband must become a loving asserter who takes full responsibility for the new relationship. Marriage is for men and women, not children.

Principle number two: *cleave.* "And shall cleave to his wife . . ." (Gen. 2:24, NASB). When a butcher cleaves, he makes two out of one. When the husband cleaves, he makes one out of two. Current attitudes toward marriage are long on romance and short on commitment. It is commitment that makes a marriage work. I must acknowledge before God and my mate that they are God's permanent provision for my incompleteness. This "cleaving" becomes the basis for a careful attending to the feelings, needs and desires of the other. It is love which has made a decision. A woman's greatest neurosis is the fear of being used and abandoned. The husband who cleaves provides the security she needs to respond with wholehearted love and devotion.

"Cleaving" is not clinging. It is not a desperate holding on to another for the sake of emotional survival. It is the act of one who chooses to be joined to another under the direction and authority of God. He sees it as a permanent commitment. As such he is willing to learn how to love, to care and to give.

Principle three: *communication*. The two "shall become one flesh" (Gen. 2:24, NASB). The sexual union in marriage is the highest form of communion, but its richness is directly related to the degree of oneness (communication) which exists in the other areas of married life. There is no such thing as not communicating in marriage. Everything which happens communicates. Silence is not always golden. A slammed door says more than a thousand words. A feigned headache may hurt the other more than multiplied words.

Unfortunately, most of us don't listen, we just monitor the conversation. Scripture says we grow to be like Christ as we speak the truth in love. We must explore feelings together if we are to build intimacy. In a marriage there is no such thing as individual victory. If I "win," I lose. If we are truly "one" our goal should always be to seek team solutions, and to work towards unanimity. Work hard on communication!

Lets summarize. A marriage is as strong as its commitments. The first and most important commitment must be to God. The new birth begins the process of the renewal of the divine image. The second commitment is to my mate. I must leave and cleave. The third is the commitment to become one flesh. Oneness establishes a permanent, exclusive, holy, redemptive union which becomes beautiful as intimacy grows through honest, caring and loving communication. "Nobody's perfect. Everything in one person nobody's got." But the person who has God has everything he needs to build the marriage. Scripture says that unless the Lord builds the house (marriage), those who build it labor in vain (see Psa. 127:1). Don't pray for the designer of marriage to overhaul your unruly mate. Nothing will happen. Instead, pray that God will make you beautiful, and look out . . . your mate will change.

Chapter 9

ROLE OF THE HUSBAND

Remember the parable of the sower and the seed? A sower went out to sow seed, and the birds devoured, the sun scorched, and the weeds choked. Likewise, two young people, full of life and love, pledged themselves to each "till death do us part," but the birds devoured, the sun scorched, the weeds choked, and death cast its shadow long before they parted. Marriage is like a garden in which one entrusts the seed of his life to the soil of the other's life. If the soil is shallow, rocky and full of choking weeds, joyous, loving, giving people can become social, emotional and spiritual cripples. Relationships deteriorate and become ugly when the potential of the seed is snuffed out by the condition of the soil. This process illustrates an important principle: *personality is the product of relationship.*

When I was a young boy, a stray German shepherd adopted us. He was incredibly fearful, and extremely wary. Any fast action or quick movement sent him scurrying away, tail between his legs. It was obvious he'd been mistreated, and because he did not know love he was very fearful. As time passed, however, love won out, and he began to change. Through a loving relationship with our family, Tex became a different dog. Personality *is* a product of relationships.

A popular song asks an important question which underscores the role relationships play in shaping personality. "Do I love you because you are beautiful, or are you beautiful because I love you?" These questions have haunted me for weeks. They really say it all. According to the song, two things exist: love and beauty. The singer is reflecting on the wonder of it all and is attempting to determine if his lover's beauty created his love, or if his love created her beauty. Although he doesn't answer his question, both statements are true.

Certainly part of love is responding to beauty, and beauty is one of love's products. Christ loves the church so that He can make it beautiful, unblemished, not having spot or wrinkle. Ultimately, people are beautiful because they have responded to someone's love. Husbands have the God given responsibilities of "loving" their wives and by so doing, making them increasingly beautiful. Unfortunately, many do not provide a healthy atmosphere for such growth to take place. Some men float the streams of life like icebergs and wonder why their wives become cool and distant. Some are like malarial swamps—poisonous, depressing and gloomy. They make life gloomy. Children stop playing when they come around. Continued exposure to a gloomy, pessimistic outlook saps the life and vitality of a joyous, spontaneous, loving wife. This chapter will look at one aspect of the husband's leadership (love) and consider its relationship to building beauty into the marriage. Wives blossom and bloom when they are secure in the love of their husbands.

If this is true, the definition of "love" becomes very important, because counterfeits cannot produce beauty, and love has its counterfeits. The Hollywood versions of love color it as a strong emotion ranging from erotic enchantment to ecstatic paralysis. They talk about "magic moments filled with love" as though it were a poetic emotion that lightens all our loads. Unfortunately, these "magic moments" have a way of becoming monotonous months filled with misery, not to mention diapers, dishes and despair. Prophets of love tell us that love is a warm feeling. The Lord told us to love those we don't like. Madison Avenue claims that the key to love is using the right toothpaste and mouthwash. The Bible focuses our attention on the cosmetics of the heart, and teaches that the *character* of the lover determines the character of his love.

Love Your Wife

In Ephesians five the husband is commanded to love his wife. It is not a suggestion, it is a command. It is impossible to command a feeling, but love as a lifestyle of action and service can be commanded. The biblical concept of love has a moral imperative behind it, and begins with an appeal to the will. Facts and action both precede and produce "feelings."

The Greek language has three words for love (*eros*, *phileo*, and *agape*) which help us understand its possibilities. These terms teach us that love involves self-satisfaction, mutual satisfaction and self-sacrifice. The first is the word *eros*, from which we get "erotic." What the Greeks sought in "eros" was total "intoxication," an ecstasy which transported them beyond rationality. Our sexuality is God's gracious provision for a unique experience of oneness which transcends "rationality." Unfortunately, this self-satisfying dimension of love is most vulnerable to distortion and abuse. Many fall in love with the "package" and not the "contents." As a result they separate function from being, and the object of their "eros" is viewed as a bearer of function rather than as a person.

Most modern-day "love" fails at this point. It desires

to devour the other person and turn him into a useful tool. Legitimate satisfaction of self easily becomes selfishness. Two people become "erotically enchanted" with each other, get married, and then discover they don't really know what love is. When "eros" is not balanced by the dimension of self-sacrifice it consumes and depersonalizes its object. Our sexuality is a God-given capacity for relationship, not exploitation. A relationship held together by *eros* without *phileo* and *agape* is inadequate because it is based on a transitory, competitive type of love. If *eros* is the only mortar of the marriage, the commitment is probably conditional. I will love you as long as you meet my needs and satisfy my desires. I will love you as long as you don't drift too far from 36-24-36. I will love you as long as the crows don't leave footprints on your face, or calories leave calling cards around your waist.

Marriage is a divine provision to meet needs. Adam needed Eve, but Eve was not a thing, a body, but a person. True love involves a responsiveness to the total self of the one loved. Marriage, therefore, is not legalized prostitution, but a relationship which involves all aspects of the personality. *Eros* becomes sacred communion only when *phileo* and *agape* are also present.

The second kind of love is *phileo*. This is the love of *mutual satisfaction* and benefit. Philadelphia is made up of the Greek word *phileo* which means "love," and *adelphos* which means "brother." It is the city of "brotherly love." *Phileo* speaks of a love which grows out of sharing the joys and sorrows of life together. Unlike *eros* which involves the ecstatic, sexual and more "irrational" dimensions of love, *phileo* speaks of the warm, affectionate, caring fellowship which can exist between two people. When a couple basks in the mutual benefits of their relationship they are experiencing *phileo* love. It is a love which recognizes and appreciates the contributions of the other.

Agape is the third dimension of love. God loves us "in

spite of" what we are and what we do. *Agape* love originates in the person loving and is not a response to the loveableness of the object. That would be *phileo* love, the love of mutual association and benefit. Scripture says "God is *agape*." He is not obligated to love, He *is* love, and He loves the whole world. Man, however, is not "love," and can only "love" if born again. Yet the new birth does not make love automatic. The command for the husband to love (*agape*) his wife introduces the element of obligation. For sinful man, *agape* is both an "in spite of" response and a response to an obligation. If "feeling" is involved, it is primarily a feeling of "obligation." This response to obligation begins in the will, not in the emotions. It says "it is my obligation to sacrifice myself and my interests in behalf of the needs of another. I will do this in obedience to God whether I feel like it or not." It is this kind of love that keeps a marriage together. This kind of love says "I will meet her needs even though I don't particularly like her at this moment."

Agape love is love that has made a decision to "cleave" for better or for worse. The husband is commanded to "agape" his wife . . . without conditioning his responsibility upon her attractiveness to him.

Love begins in the will and moves to the emotions. Genuine *agape* leads to *phileo* and makes *eros* sacred communion.

Priorities in Love

The Greeks have helped us define love; let's look now at its *priorities* before we consider its practice. If I am beautiful because I've responded to love, and God *is* love, then my relationship to him is my number one priority.

This is why the spiritual leadership of the husband is so

crucial. If he cultivates a relationship with the Lord, his capacity and ability to love his wife will be greatly increased. If he is regularly, daily, functioning as a priest for his family, his family will reap the benefits of unity, love and rich fellowship. The husband needs to be secure in God's love for him if he is going to be able to love his wife and family. If God doesn't love me, I can't love myself. If He doesn't care about me, why should I? If I'm not important to Him, does it matter if I'm important to anyone else? But He does care, He does love me. I am important to Him. He knows my name. I am to love God with all my heart, and love my neighbor in the same way I love myself. But I can't love my neighbor—the one "nigh" to me—if I don't love myself. I can't love myself if I don't love God. The first priority is love of God.

God has made full provision in Christ to deal with my impurity and guilt which makes me hate myself. He forgives me, and so must I. He knows fully, and yet plants me in the soil of His love. So how do I love God? True religion is not divine apple polishing, it is the careful cultivation of a relationship. The ultimate expression of my love for God is obedience. As John Newton said, my ultimate goal should be "to do all for Him, to find all in Him, and to receive all from Him." If I obey Him I do what He desires. What He desires is always an expression of His character. If I do what He desires I express His character. Beauty is the possession and expression of His character. If I love him, I obey. If I obey, I'm beautiful. If I'm growing in beauty so can my wife and children, because personality is the product of relationships. The issue of love's first priority is *allegiance*.

The second priority of love is learning to *love yourself*. Here we wrestle with the problem of *acceptance*. We must believe what God has said. He has posted the garbage heap of our past with "no trespassing" signs. We must never allow the evil one to lead us into the past and engage us in "sifting garbage." God knows us fully, even before we tell

Him how we feel or think. He knows every intimate detail about us and still considers us infinitely valuable to Him. He has seen us at our worst. He has read our thoughts and seen our motives when they were cruel, angry, jealous and full of hatred. He understands us even in our most degrading moments and still chooses to love us. We must see ourselves from *His* point of view. When we accept ourselves, it enables us to be ashamed without being discouraged, to accept blame without forming unhealthy attitudes about ourselves. It also allows us to accept our limitations. We must not hate what He loves. To do so is sin.

The third priority for us is to *love our neighbors*. Loving God leads to spiritual maturity. The spiritually mature person is one who has learned to love himself. Loving himself is the key to emotional maturity and frees one to love his fellow man . . . or his wife!

In each of the priorities of love, the facts, when accepted and acted upon, produce the feelings. The facts of God's love, acceptance, forgiveness and care produce the feelings of appreciation, admiration, adoration and affection. If I do not acknowledge the facts and act upon them, I will not experience the feelings. Our emotions are the products of our thoughts.

Practice of Love

Having considered the possibilities and the priorities of love, we now will consider the *practice* of love, especially as it relates to the role of the husband. Love is like electricity: we're not sure what it is, but we can show you what it does. The foremost responsibility of the husband is to *love his wife* in the same way Christ loves the church.

We may not know for sure what love is, but Christ enables us to see what it does. From His example we learn some important principles which enable the marriage relationship to be a display case for His character.

First, *love makes the beauty of the other its primary concern*. Christ's love sets beauty as its goal, and assumes the responsibility of taking whatever measure necessary to procure it. "Husbands, love your wives, as Christ loved the church and gave himself up for her, that he might sanctify her, having cleansed her by the washing of water with the word, that he might present the church to himself in splendor, without spot or wrinkle or any such thing, that she might be holy and without blemish" (Eph. 5:25-27, RSV).

The word "sanctify" describes the goal or intention of Christ' love. The word means to set apart unto holiness or "wholeness." Christ's desire is that His relationship to the church would enable her to be presented before Him in splendor, holy and without blemish. The husband's love is to enrich the totality of his wife's life. Love's goal must be the "wholeness" of the other.

"Cleansing" describes the process which accomplishes the goal of wholeness. In the case of Christ, it involves the provision of all that is necessary to set one free from impurity and move him towards beauty. Our Lord literally "gave himself up" for the church's beauty.

Second, love *sacrifices self for the beauty of the other*. Christ loved the church and gave Himself up for her. The church is moving toward beauty because He loves it. This is where the rubber hits the pavement. Aren't I the head? The boss? The king? Isn't my wife to submit, to obey, to serve, to be *my* "helpmate"? The Bible says Christ is the pattern. He gave Himself up. He emptied himself of the free exercise of His position power and became a servant to the church, His body. He functioned as a Saviour/Servant. Who can resist a servant, one who comes to meet needs, to give unselfishly of his time and talent to meet the needs of another? The husband who "gives himself up" is the one who puts the physical, emotional, and spiritual needs of his wife above his own needs.

Finally, love *provides a healthy soil in which the other can grow toward beauty.* A husband is to nourish and cherish his wife in the same way Christ "nourishes and cherishes" the church (Eph. 5:29, RSV). The word "nourish" means to provide all the nutrients necessary for growth. "Cherish" literally means "to warm." A rosebud needs two things to open up and reveal its inner beauty: the nourishment of the soil and the warmth of the sun. Is your wife beautiful because you love her? If you love her she will be beautiful. She needs two things to reveal beauty. First, nourishment. Second, warmth and tenderness. Is beauty your goal? Are you willing to sacrifice yourself to accomplish it? She has planted her life in the soil of your life. Do yourself a favor, love your wife.

Chapter 10

A BEAUTIFUL
SPIRIT

I spent a summer on a Forest Service lookout by myself and nearly starved to death! Cooking just isn't my thing. I got to be pretty good at making blueberry pancakes, however. Each morning I'd walk down to the spring below the lookout to get some water. The spring was surrounded with wild blueberries which I reluctantly shared with the bears. They ate them leaves and all. I was a little more discriminating. Usually I'd break off a branch and take it to the lookout and pick the berries and drop them directly into the batter. Slathered with homemade butter and bathed in syrup, the resulting pancakes were delightful. Thank God for Aunt Jemima. I trusted her to have all the right ingredients mixed together in the proper portions. All I had to do was add milk and blueberries.

Wouldn't you love to see a box on the supermarket shelf which said "Instant Marriage, just add water." Most marriage partners could probably agree on the basic ingredients for a marriage recipe; the problem is one of proportion and emphasis. The husband lobbies loudly for submission as an essential ingredient, but is somewhat agnostic when it comes to spiritual leadership and sacrificial love. The wife may picket for leadership, responsibility and security but play down reverence, humility and a quiet spirit. A cake is not really worth eating unless it has the right ingredients in the proper proportion. Sugar is wonderful, but too much will ruin a recipe. A husband who equates headship with bull-headedness may be able to demand response, but he cannot demand respect. The wife whose husband follows Peter's admonition to honor her finds the joyful acceptance of his leadership an easy gift to give him.

Why Submit?

In this chapter we want to consider the meaning and significance of submission and see how it contributes to the beauty of the marriage relationship. So why submission? First of all, *submission is necessary so that a man can be a man.* An old proverb says "Ill fares the house that knows a rooster that's silent and a hen that crows."

God holds the man responsible to exercise intelligent supportive leadership. There cannot be two leaders. "Subjection" is a military term and signifies a "standing under" the rank or position power of another being. Although the husband has been delegated position-power, his role as savior/servant puts the greatest emphasis on person-power. How he uses his position is carefully prescribed in Christ's example of sacrificial love for the church of which He is the head.

In I Corinthians 11:7 Paul declares that a woman is the glory of man. To say that a woman is man's glory is one of the most beautiful compliments a woman can receive. Because she bears the image of God, she is able to be the glory of man. Each sex contributes to and complements the other by being wholly other. Women need to be women so that men can be men. Men must be men if women are going to be women. It is man as man, joined to woman as woman, that most accurately reflects the glory and majesty of God. In maleness the loving authority of God is made visible. The nurturing, compassionate and loving attributes of God are made visible through femaleness. To blurr, hide or distort these qualities is to mar the very image of God.

One of the essential ingredients of manhood is leadership. He looks for a cave with a bear in it and wants to risk everything to drive the bear out of the cave. Doesn't sound like your husband? Although men have differing degrees of leadership ability at a given point in their lives, nearly all men want to risk themselves to accomplish something. If a wife destroys the early attempts of her husband's leadership, fumbling as they may be, she destroys part of his manhood and diminishes her love and respect for him. Remember that the principle of personality being a product of relationship works both ways. Paul tells us that a woman is to reverence her husband (see Eph. 5:33). This means she is to believe in him, to be his number one supporter. This encourages his leadership ability and increases her respect and admiration for him.

Second, submission is the *key to a woman being a woman*. God has defined maleness and femaleness. Only as we work within His framework can we be fully man and woman. Submission is not inferiority, it is subordination. We live in an ordered universe in which authority and submission must exist. All authority comes from God. He has established several authority-submission relationships for humanity. Every person has more than one authority-submission relationship in his life. For example, children are to obey parents. Employees are to submit to employers. Citizens are to obey their government.

Paul says that the woman is to be subject to her husband as unto the Lord. (see Eph. 5:22). The Lord is pleased when a woman acknowledges and responds to her husband's leadership.

Third, *submission provides the most risk-free context for the expression of the husband's love.* Let's face it, love is risky because whenever we genuinely give of ourselves we risk rejection and failure. It is not natural or easy for most men to love anyone, much less their wives. Submission is an attitude which encourages love, which lowers the risk of giving sacrificially. The wife who encourages her husband's leadership by her words and deeds does herself a great favor. She thereby acknowledges that she has withdrawn from competition for "leadership," and the husband is no longer threatened. Competitive relationships make submission and love very difficult. Submission sets the stage for a complementary relationship and encourages the pilgrimage to genuine oneness. The submission of the wife is designed to stimulate the love of the husband. The husband's love is designed to stimulate the wife's submission. When both are fulfilling their responsibilities, harmony, unity and beauty are clearly seen.

Having seen that submission is the key to man being man and woman being woman, let's look at some further insights on the subject from Peter.

Peter's Insights

The book of I Peter breaks down very nicely into three topics: salvation, submission and suffering. The heart of his letter deals with the subject of submission. The main idea of his extended discussion is that submission is so unusual and so beautiful that it calls attention to the presence of God in human experience. Servants are to be subject to masters—even tyrants—with the hope that the godliness of the servant will result in his master turning to God. Christ is singled out as the example for both the servant and the wife (see I Pet. 2:21). Notice that I Peter 3:1 begins by saying "In the same way, you wives, be submissive . . ." (NASB).

"In the same way" refers back to Christ's example in chapter two. His example illustrates at least three crucial principles. Let's look at verses 21-23.

> "For you have been called for this purpose, since Christ also suffered for you, leaving you an example for you to follow in His steps, who committed no sin, nor was any deceit found in His mouth; and while being reviled, He did not revile in return; while suffering, He uttered no threats, but kept entrusting Himself to Him who judges righteously . . ." NASV.

Principle number one: *Treatment does not determine temperament.* When Christ was reviled, He didn't respond in kind. We are to follow His example. This means that when hubby growls like a grizzly, wife is not to growl back. Christ bore the full force of man's inhumanity as an innocent victim. When attacked verbally, He held His tongue. When abused physically, He controlled His actions. The Bible doesn't say, "Be submissive provided your husband treats you right." Chances are he won't.

Christ not only submitted, but He cared enough for His executioners that He prayed for their forgiveness. Some women are obedient, but not submissive in the true sense. Some go by the letter of the law and not the spirit of it. A child can be disobedient and told to sit in a corner. He may be sitting down on the outside and yet standing up on the inside. Ultimately the issue of authority must be settled in one's relationship to God. A woman "standing up on the inside" probably has not settled the issue of God's authority in her life. Furthermore, she can't hide her "standing up on the inside" attitudes. In effective communication only 7 percent is verbal; 38 percent is tone of voice and 55 percent is non-verbal. A slammed door, a turned shoulder and clenched teeth get the message across clearly. So how do you respond to mistreatment and misunderstanding? Not with more of the same.

The second principle helps us understand how the first is possible. *There is a third party to every action and reaction.* Christ committed Himself to Him who judges justly. A number of important concepts are locked up in this principle. A judge presupposes judgment according to a standard. It suggests that there is someone observing who serves as a source of motivation and comfort. He *is* observing every action and reaction. This alone should motivate one to respond properly. Furthermore, the one who observes also understands. He knows our intentions even if misunderstood and misrepresented by another. The divine observer also is a sustainer, one whose strength is made perfect in our weakness. Finally, the observer also has access to the life and conscience of the one who mistreats another. When a wife refuses to respond to ugliness with ugliness, the Spirit of God is freed to appeal directly to the conscience of the offender. When we love our enemies we "heap coals of fire" (conviction) upon their heads (see Rom. 12:20).

A third principle helps us understand the *power* of submission. It states that *the ultimate objective is worth the cost.* Christ's submission resulted in His bearing our sins on the cross so that we might be set free to live a life of right relationships (see I Pet. 2:24). In verse 25 Peter closes his discussion of Christ's example by reminding his readers that many of them had been straying like sheep, but now have returned unto the "Shepherd and Bishop of their souls" (KJV). Christ won! His seeming defeat was a victory. His submission resulted in straying sheep discovering the true Shepherd and Bishop of their souls. The centurion saw Christ submit to His captors, love a thief on a cross, and pray for His executioners. It spoke to him. He wasn't used to people dying this way. His comment: "Truly this was the Son of God" (Matt. 27:54, KJV).

Peter says, "In the same way, you wives, be submissive to your own husbands so that even if any of them are disobedient to the word they may be won without a word by the behavior of their wives" (II Pet. 3:1, NASB). Men often complain that their wives have lost their beauty and attractiveness, the very qualities which the husband's love is to sustain and develop. Wives often complain about their husbands' lack of leadership and spiritual maturity, the very thing their submission and inner beauty are designed to stimulate. Godly submission stimulates godly leadership.

In chapter three Peter sets forth a *principle* in verses 1-2, describes the *practice* of submission in verses 3-4, and then suggests a *pattern* for submission in verses 5-7. He is providing a "do-it-yourself kit" for wives which enables them to have a vital part in developing the leadership abilities of their husbands.

First the *principle* of verses 1-2. The principle is, "Win him without a word." It is your walk, not your talk; your life, not your lip, which will serve as a catalyst to his development. If your husband is disobedient to God's Word, what makes you think he will listen to yours? Nagging may produce change, but it will always be at the expense of the relationship. The root of the word "nag" comes from an old Anglo-Saxon term which means "to gnaw." It pictures a mouse gnawing away on a rope, one bite at a time. Ben Sira, an ancient writer, said, "A loud crying woman and a nag shall be sought out to drive away enemies."

Notice what *does* communicate. They may be won when they "observe your chaste and respectful behavior" (v. 2, NASB). The word "see" in the original text is not a "quick glance" but rather a thorough evaluation. Peter says two things will capture their attention. First, when they see behavior which is *chaste*, that is pure and innocent, free of ulterior motives and subtle manipulation. Second, when they sense behavior which is *reverent*, Peter says they will take notice. We reverence something when we acknowledge its proper place in the scheme of things and respond appropriately. It's the opposite of belittling someone or putting him down. Wives sometimes say "I wish my husband would be the leader in our home." I remind them that he *is* the leader. The position is his by divine decree. His practice or exercise of his position is what is apparently lacking. However, the woman who reverences her husband because of his *position* as head will discover the key to helping him *practice* his headship. Lip service to his headship is irreverent.

The Practice of Submission

The practice of submission is described in verses 3-4. "And let not your adornment be external only—braiding the hair, and wearing gold jewelry, and putting on dresses; but let it be the hidden person of the heart, with the imperishable quality of a gentle and quiet spirit, which is precious in the sight of God" (NASB). He begins with a negative. Don't focus your efforts on outward adornment only. A beautiful hairstyle, flashy jewelry and lovely clothes are not the key to stimulating your husband's leadership qualities. There is no garment which can cover a critical, rebellious heart. Peter suggests that a change of clothes is not the best way to call attention to a change of heart. If outward external appearance is all a woman has to offer, most men have secretaries or associates who are better competition.

Peter is certainly not suggesting that Christians should look dowdy. They should be the most beautiful people in the world! He is reminding us that beauty is not primarily external. Many wives have sinned against their husbands by letting themselves become sloppy and physically unattractive.

The positive dimension of submission is the commitment to grow in inner beauty. Peter says that submission involves adorning the hidden person of the heart "with the imperishable quality of a gentle and quiet spirit, which is precious in the sight of God" (v. 4, NASB).

God doesn't give us too many clues as to what is precious in His estimations. In God's estimation a gentle and quiet spirit is considered like an imperishable jewel.

One of the evidences of love is the desire to please the other, to discover what they value, to provide what they need, to be what brings delight to them. God's heart is warmed, He is delighted when a woman's submission is exhibited through a gentle and quiet spirit. God says it's beautiful. Such women win all the awards in His fashion shows.

Our Lord is the prime example of a quiet and gentle spirit. As we observed in an earlier chapter, Jesus was able to become a "towel wearer and basin bearer" for His disciples because He was secure in His position before God and in the scheme of things. He in no way was suggesting He was inferior, quite the opposite. The disciples were sure they were inferior, and as a result couldn't submit and serve. Our Lord linked greatness with humility, declaring that the one who would be great must become a servant to all.

The Trinity is our pattern for humility. In John 17, Christ prays that we will live in unity following the pattern of the Trinity (see v. 21). God is seen as the chief administrator or the "head executive." Christ is sent under His authority to fulfill His purposes. The Holy Spirit submerges His identity and seeks to exalt the person of Christ.

Even though Christ has the greatest "visibility," He subordinates himself to the Father. The Holy Spirit uses His resources to exalt the being of Christ and focus the world's attention upon Him. Is there submission in the Trinity? Yes. Is there subordination of relationship? Yes. Is there division of responsibility? Yes. Is one more important than the others? No. Is one superior to the others? Of course not, there is total equality. Is man appointed as the leader because of an inherent superiority? Is the woman to submit because she is inferior? Did Christ submit himself to His executioners because He was inferior? No, it was part of the Master's master plan. So is the leadership of the husband and the submission of the wife. *God* says such behavior is beautiful. I believe it.

This passage tells me that submission is *the* mark of maturity for a Christian wife. Not her church activities, her faithful attendance at this study or that ministry function, but her willing acceptance and encouragement of her husband's leadership. In a very real sense, beautiful women get what they want. They "rule" by submission. Ladies, you are irresistable when you're beautiful, and God and men think genuine, gracious, feminine reverence is beautiful.

Sarah, Abraham's wife, is singled out for the pattern of submission in verses 5-6. "For in this way in former times the holy women also, who hoped in God, used to adorn themselves, being submissive to their own husbands. Thus Sarah obeyed Abraham, calling him lord, and you have become her children if you do what is right without being frightened by any fear" (NASB). Notice what Peter says about Sarah. First, like Christ, she "hoped in God." She recognized the sovereignty of God in human relationships. Hope is crucial isn't it? When things are rough, if we have hope, there's light at the end of the tunnel. Hope enables us to endure. For the "joy" (hope) which was set before Him, Christ endured the cross (see Heb. 12:2). Sarah first "hoped in God." Faith is vital to wholehearted submission. Because she "hoped in God," she was able to adorn (beautify) herself by being in submission to Abraham. Note again that beauty (adornment) is directly related to submission.

Peter says that she obeyed Abraham, calling him lord. Two things are underscored in that statement. First, she submitted (obeyed); second, she reverenced him, calling him lord. I don't believe God desires wives to run around

116

bowing and scraping and calling their husbands "lord." It's a matter of attitude. There is no reason to question the sincerity which lay behind Sarah's use of "lord" as a title for her husband.

At this point some might say, "If I were married to Abraham, it would be easy to submit to him. Whatever my husband is, he's not an Abraham." Actually, Abraham left much to be desired as a husband. Sarah was beautiful, and Abraham feared that some sheik would like to add her to his harem. He, like modern man, found a loophole and used it. Sarah was not only his wife, but his half-sister. On two occasions, her beauty caught the attention of an ardent suitor and Abraham, fearing for his life, passed her off as his sister. Is it any wonder she "hoped in God?" Peter declares that the woman who follows Sarah's example becomes a member of her sorority.

Christ is the pattern of the husband's love and the wife's submission. Submission is a divine beauty secret. Divine in that it is revealed to be beautiful by God and beautiful because it reveals God. Do yourself a favor: stimulate your husband's leadership by being a supportive follower.

Chapter 11

THE BEAUTY OF PARENT-CHILD RELATIONSHIPS

Bees have always fascinated me. When I was a youngster on the farm my brothers and I discovered a bee's nest in the ground. The entrance was located in a steep bank alongside a country road. The bees were flying in and out of the entrance to their underground home, apparently oblivious to their discovery by four curious and mischievous farm boys. Someone suggested it might be fun to clamp a bottle over the entrance and trap the bees in the ground. It was. An old Kerr bottle worked perfectly. We stuck it over the entrance and put some cement around it to hold it in place. The bottle served as sort of an "aquarium for bees." The bees coming out of the ground found themselves confined in a quart jar. We could watch them and they could watch us, and yet we were safe from their venom. The bottle soon filled up with swarming bees. I'm sure their traffic control tower officers committed suicide.

Picture it if you will. Here we were, sitting on the ground laughing at the trapped bees and our cleverness when one of my brothers grabbed a stick and shattered the bottle. That wasn't too clever. All of a sudden these lovely bees who were conforming so beautifully to our plans turned into supercharged kamikaze pilots bent on destruction. They were totally unreasonable. An appeal to the United Nations Security Council wouldn't have fazed them. Licking our wounds, we concluded that if you want honey, you don't kick over the bee hive. Why do the lessons of life have to be so painful at times?

Children trapped in a glass bottle conform nicely—until the bottle breaks. And then that sweet young thing becomes an insatiable monster. When circumstances are right, their real nature appears. Parenting is tough. It's a lot easier for parents to have children than it is for children to have parents. Parenting is tough, because marriage is tough. Storms are raging on many home fronts, and life's weather forecasters predict continued cloudiness with a good possibility of further thundershowers.

When marital conflict generates emotional lightning storms, the child usually becomes the lightning conductor. Personality is the product of relationships. Parents are psychological mirrors for their children, and the child is shaped by the image of himself he sees reflected in his parents. I'm certain every parent sincerely desires to have "beautiful" children. I'm not so sure most of them have thought a lot about the nature of beauty. For many parents the beautiful child is the "model" child, which is to say, the child who doesn't make waves, who keeps quiet, who doesn't interfere with the parents' plans. Usually "model" children are neither happy nor self-regulating.

Moses on Parenting

We *do* want beautiful children, but there's a price to be paid. Moses sets it out for us in Deuteronomy chapter 6. Deuteronomy contains five sermons Moses delivered just prior to his death. The children of Israel are about to enter the promised land under the able leadership of Joshua. Forty years of wandering in the Sinai wilderness eliminated the older generation, those who could remember the slavery in Egypt. Moses has a great concern for the second generation, "fair weather" believers. They are a young, excited group about to enter God's promised land. They are about to dwell in cities and homes they didn't build, use cisterns they didn't dig, and harvest the bounty of vineyards and olive groves they didn't plant. Suddenly they will move from poverty to prosperity. Moses is concerned about how faith in Jehovah will be transmitted from generation to generation in this new environment with its unique set of circumstances. Moses is aware that adversity tends to focus men's thoughts on God whereas prosperity encourages men to neglect the very one who makes prosperity possible. Verse 10 through 12 expresses Moses' concern.

> "Then it shall come about when the Lord your God brings you into the land which He swore to your fathers, Abraham, Isaac and Jacob, to give you, great and splendid cities which you did not build, and houses full of all good things which you did not fill, and hewn cisterns which you did not dig, vineyards and olive trees which you did not plant, and you shall eat and be satisfied, then watch yourself, lest you forget the Lord who brought you from the land of Egypt, out of the house of slavery" (NASB).

How quickly we forget to remember, especially when life is good, and things seem to be going well. But Moses is concerned with more than memory about God's dealings in the past. He is concerned about how faith, trust and dependence can be fostered in a context which on the surface seems to have made such qualities obsolete. When the barns are full, the bank statement is healthy, and living is easy, faith is tough. The problem is compounded when we

121

reflect on the fact that faith is caught and not taught.

I was raised on a small farm. As a result chores were part of my everyday experience. There were cows to milk, calves to feed, barns to clean, fences to mend, gardens to plant and weed, trees to prune, hay to cut and put in the barn. If you forgot to close the gate, the cows visited the garden. If you neglected to clean out the loafing shed, you milked a dirty cow the next morning. And the cows had to be milked *every* morning whether it was convenient or not. The experience of living on a farm had lots of "education" built into it. We learned to use tools, operate farm equipment, feed and care for animals, and plant, cultivate and harvest all kinds of crops. We didn't learn these skills because we particularly wanted to, we did it by necessity. If we didn't cut wood in fall, there was no heat in the winter. If we didn't dig the potatoes and store them in bins, we went without. If we didn't churn the cream, there was no butter. The growing and living cycles of farm life were built-in, extrinsically motivated educational experiences.

But I don't live in the country anymore. There are no more tractors to repair, fences to mend, crops to plant, cows, pigs, chickens, ducks and rabbits to care for. My little boy, Stephen, is probably going to grow up and be a "city-slicker." I find it much more difficult to teach him responsibility and appreciation in beautiful Newport Beach, California. It is difficult to structure experiences which are not "contrived" or "artificial." A regular and adequate paycheck makes it more difficult to teach him faith. It's one thing to talk about it, it's quite another thing to live by it.

My dad's salary seldom covered the needs of nine children. Raising our food wasn't a luxury, it was a matter of survival. Much of our clothing came from the local "missionary barrel." I can remember cutting cardboard "feet" to put inside my shoes to keep the water from coming through the holes in the sole. In this kind of environment, trust in God was a necessity, and we saw Him provide in wonderful ways. As a result I have been privileged to learn some significant lessons about faith. Stephen, my wonderful six-year-old, takes for granted many of the very things we trusted God for each month. Somehow telling him that "God provides it" isn't the same as actually seeing God provide a car when there is no money to buy one or provide clothing when it is not available, or funds to build on a room for grandma after grandpa died.

Moses' "blueprint for beauty" begins with setting forth a crucial perspective which is the foundational principle of a Godly home. "Hear, O Israel! The Lord is our God, the Lord is one! And you shall love the Lord your God with all your heart and with all your soul and with all your might" (Deut 6:4-5, NASB). In the New Testament, Jesus adds, "Thou shalt love thy neighbor as thyself" (Matt. 22:39, KJV).

Scripture teaches us that where our treasure is, there will our heart be also (see Matt. 6:21). Stephen's heart right now is at the toy store because they carry the model airplanes he loves so much. He eats, sleeps and talks about airplanes. Any money he can get his hands on goes towards another model. He uses every conceivable resource to convince us that we should take him to the toy store. He's a very effective "evangelist" for the model airplane market. I'm certain his love for planes has no relationship to the fact that his father buys every magazine on flying he can get his hands on.

The command of Moses to love God with the totality of our being is not unfamiliar to most of us as a concept. We've heard it many times. Moses is saying that a fervent, wholehearted love for God is the only effective antidote to the influences of this life. An all-out love for Him is the key to coping with pain and adjusting to prosperity. The dangers of both are averted by a fervent love for the Saviour. In the case of God, to love is to obey, to obey is to do, to do God's will is to display His character, to display His character is to be beautiful. Man's love for God is the only legitimate motive or principle for human action. If we are motivated by our love for God we are serving with eternal values in view. It's a great and glorious concept which is easy to discuss and difficult to do because we aren't lovers by nature. Although most of us couldn't be convicted in court for loving God supremely, it is the desire of many hearts. It's a goal, a target, a direction, a perspective which is essential to raising a generation, a family, a household who are committed to the same pursuit.

Building Love into Family Life

Life is filled with the good and the best, with tensions between conflicting priorities. Up to this point Moses is saying that the one who would transmit life and beauty must come to grips with the crucial doctrine of loving God supremely. Having enumerated the crucial doctrine, Moses points out the process by which love of God becomes a part of the lifestyle of our families. The first step that he underscores is that God's truth, this concept of loving God supremely, must *be responded to with the heart*. Notice verse 6 "And these words, which I am commanding you today, shall be on your heart" (NASB). He's speaking primarily to parents and reminding them that if the truth about loving God supremely has not rooted itself in their hearts, they have not taken the most crucial step toward building God's principles of life into their children. The child must sense that the motive for doing right is a deep love for a living being, not a legalistic adherence to an ecclesiastical code. It is easy to do all the right things for the wrong reasons. Loving God supremely must be a settled conviction of your heart. All other idols must be banished, all other competing loyalties must be subordinated. You must acknowledge Him as Lord, and live out the reality of that confession in human experience. The motive for such a direction of affection is the reality of His love and of His desire that we be enriched, blessed and fulfilled. Because He loves us, He wills our growth, our maturity, our fulfillment. Willing obedience to God is a logical response to His personal concerns for us. He is for us! Our love for God should not be of necessity, although it is a necessity.

The child raised in such an environment senses the spirit of the parent long before he can understand his parents' words. The child tends to pattern himself after the parents' attitudes and actions. He usually ignores the parents' admonitions. Moses puts his finger on the key to beauty in the home: the beauty of the heart of a parent in holy pursuit of God. What direction are you going? The direction of the heart is determined by its desired destination. God and His purposes are to be the magnetic north pole of the believer's life. When this is true, his children catch the "real disease."

In verse 7, Moses points out that his concept of loving God supremely is to be *perpetuated in the home*. What begins in the heart must be lived out in the environment of the home. Home is the place above all else where we learn the high cost of loving. Life's most crucial curriculum is *still* taught in the home. Notice Moses' words: "And you shall teach them diligently to your sons and shall *talk* of them when you sit in your house and when you walk by the way and when you lie down and when you rise up" (NASB, italics added). What a significant verse!

The phrase "teach them diligently" is used of a farmer taking a dull instrument and sharpening it by repeated grinding. The idea of repetition is at the heart of its meaning. It suggests one dimension of the educational task which involves teaching again and again as one takes a blunt instrument and whets it by repeated friction and grinding. Frequency and consistency of instruction seems to lie at the heart of the concept. In our culture we would probably link Moses' instruction with some kind of a "family altar" or family worship experience. The emphasis would appear to be upon a regular, systematic, formal type of educational experience.

My experience as a child underscores the value of such an educational experience. Every morning and evening Dad led us in the reading of the Word and prayer. Every morning and evening! Nine children! Nine wiggly, squirming, bickering children. I must confess I still marvel at this fact. I don't know how my parents pulled it off. All our meals began and ended with prayer. No one left the table until we had come together into the presence of the Lord. Many of my fondest memories go back to times around the dinner table. It wasn't until I was in graduate school that I learned that what happens at the dinner table is probably the most significant influence in the life of the child.

Many people were subjected to "family worship" and experienced a very negative result. Some who have been thus exposed still have a difficult time reading the Word because of bad associations from childhood. Obviously there are dangers involved in such educational endeavors. The danger of a "formal" instructional time is "formalism." The child can misinterpret the intention of the family worship and become very "form conscious." He begins to believe that the important thing in life is to observe the forms, the traditions of the Christian faith. His level of commitment is measured by his exercise of the "forms." He may come to believe that if he reads and prays every day he's functioning as a mature Christian. He falls into the trap of going through the forms without the reality. The end result can be ugly—a child who "knows the answers," but hasn't had the experience. "Formalism" often produces sterility, ritual without reality. The more formal "family worship" is not enough. The danger is not so much content as it is *context*. Truth is not to be taught in isolation from life.

Moses goes on to explain an informal context for teaching which makes the content of a more formal session meaningful. In the formal teaching situation the parent functions primarily as an interpreter of God's principles of life as seen in Scripture. The informal opportunities for teaching link those principles with the everyday experiences. Notice again Moses' words: "You shall talk of them when you sit in your house and when you walk by the way and when you lie down and when you rise up."

The normal events of the day provide an excellent context for helping children learn to love God supremely, to link the Word of God to the current experience of the child. A beautiful sunset, a trip to the mountains, the death of a pet, the normal pains and joys of life become teachable moments. The needs of the family become great opportunities to teach faith and trust. I appreciate so much the fact that my parents shared their financial needs with us and allowed us to pray with them and share the joy of God's provision.

Moses is not suggesting that the parent get on his soap box and moralize when a "teachable moment" arises. He seems to be suggesting that discussion about God and His basic principles of life should be a normal part of daily conversation. When we are sitting together in the den, lying on the couch, playing in the yard, walking to the park, driving in the car, we can share life together in such a way that God's principles are set forth in conversation and illustrated by example. Mother taught all of us children to be observers of beauty. As we would drive through the country she would call attention to the beauty of a stream, the interesting texture of a tree's bark, the symmetry of its leaves, the shape of the clouds and many other facets of God's glorious creation. To this day I see God's footprints everywhere because mother talked of God when we "walked by the way."

The word "talk" suggests that the Word of God is to be

talked about. Moses is suggesting that talk about God should be a part of our everyday conversation. Unfortunately, many misuse God's Word, and successfully immunize their children against it. God never intended it to be used as a club to instill fear. The key to introducing the family to God's love is for it to be the driving force of the parents' life. When dad milked the cows he would put a stand in the gutter and read from the Scriptures. This went on for years until I was old enough to milk the cows. For six or seven years I too read several chapters each morning while milking the cows. Why? Because dad told me to? Because the Word demanded it? Because dad did it? I did it because of what my father was as a person. My motivation did not grow out of his position as president of a college, as father of nine children, or because he had a Th.D after his name. He lived a balanced, godly life. He lived what he believed and he practiced what he professed. We knew that the time spent in the Word was valuable because we had a perpetual visual aid of its beautifying effect on the lives of our parents.

Beauty is not skin deep. "Skin deep" beauty is seen for what it is and rejected by children. The truth of loving God supremely is to be modeled in the life of the parents. How they respond to people, circumstances and responsibilities, the choices they make, the priorities they pursue, the values they live by all serve to indicate the true condition of their faith. When children are exposed to godly models, the formal and informal learning experiences have credibility. That which comes from the heart reaches the heart. What Moses is saying is "train up a child in the way he should go, and walk there once in awhile yourself." Practice doesn't make perfect, it makes permanent. The process of perpetuating beauty begins with a beautiful heart. This beauty provides the right context for teaching God's principles of life in the home. That which begins in the parents *hearts* is to be perpetuated in the *home*.

Building Habits

Moses takes us one step further and suggests that the parents' job is not complete until the concept of loving God supremely is exhibited in the family's *habit patterns*. To know and not to do is not to know at all. Notice verses 8 and 9, "And you shall bind them as a sign on your hand and they shall be as frontals on your forehead. And you shall write them on the doorposts of your house and on your gates" (NASB). Moses is suggesting that our love for God is to be expressed in every facet of our life. The phrase "bound upon your hands" suggests that every time our hand reaches out to perform an action it is controlled by the desire to love God supremely. We are to ask ourselves, "Will this action reflect the fact that I love God supremely?" Moses is suggesting that outward control without inner conviction is deadly. Children who have a sufficient rationale for rules find rules to be reasonable. If mom and dad are progressing in their love and commitment to God, and the children love their parents, they too will come to share in their parents' desires.

Moses' use of the phrase "and they shall be as frontals on your forehead" suggests that the concept of loving God supremely must rule in our thought life. We become what we perceive ourselves to be. Change comes by restructuring a new mental image of the person we are intended to be. When we visualize ourselves as persons who are to love God supremely and set that as a goal, everything changes. Our affections must be set on heavenly things. Every thought must be brought into captivity to Christ. Garbage must go. We can't afford to feed our minds on garbage because we never sin in isolation. Our families often pay the cost for our lack of discipline in this crucial area. Dirty minds do not produce beautiful families. Impurity contaminates love. Only those who avoid darkness and walk in the light have fellowship with God. If the faith is to be preserved intact from generation to generation, parents must allow their commitment to love God supremely to rule their thought lives.

Moses' references to the "doorposts of the house" suggests that the concept of loving God supremely is to permeate all that happens in the family unit. What a challenge! To love as God loves, to give as God gives, to forgive as God forgives, to discipline as God disciplines. My goal as a parent is to have everyone in the family unit committed to allowing God's love to reign in human relationships. If it's not true in the parents' hearts, it probably won't be true in the home.

The last area in which this concept of loving God supremely is to be lived out or modeled is in the business world. The term "gates" is synonomous with the business community. Moses is calling for total consistency in every area of life. What a challenge! If a vital faith is to be perpetuated from generation to generation we can't be one thing at home and something else at the office. A double standard is not only inconsistent with loving God supremely, it cannot be hidden because it is part of the person living that way. Children pick it up quickly, and become imitators of their parents.

Moses' sermon illustrates that the motivation for proper actions, clean thoughts and a healthy home life is not an authoritarian, domineering father, but instead, the love of God. The one who loves God to the best of his ability and understanding cares how he acts, how he thinks and how he relates in the home and business community. There are some important principles which grow out of Moses' strategy for perpetuating beauty and goodness. First, *rules follow principles*. The child who has accepted God's principles of life is better prepared to accept the fact that "freedom has fences." When the child submits himself to God, the source of values, he is better prepared to accept his parents' rules and regulations. He has a rationale for rules when the principles of God have been internalized. Rules tell us *what* to do, but it's only a clear appreciation of God's character which tell us *why* we need to do it. Rules without an adequate rationale often produce bitterness and resentment.

Second, the parent is to serve as an *interpreter of life*. This may take place in the ordinary events of the day. God provides many opportunities for parents to invest everyday events with divine significance. An interpreter is a person who knows a different language and can make sense out of sounds which are meaningless to others. The child sees, hears and is involved in many things which he either cannot understand or misunderstands. A loving, sensitive parent has the privilege of taking such "teachable moments" and relating them to a divine, eternal perspective. This process presupposes time and interest. It means being with children, entering their world and becoming naturalized citizens. The average father spends less than seven minutes per week alone with his son, and wonders why there is a "generation gap."

A third principle: *when the zest goes, the rest goes*. Faith, love and beauty are contagious. So are indifference, selfishness and immaturity. Immaturity breeds immaturity. Lack of discipline breeds lack of discipline. Enthusiasm breeds enthusiasm. A vibrant, growing, caring, whole-hearted love for God produces a desire for a vibrant, growing, caring, whole-hearted love for God. In a very real sense we can "Love God and do as we please." William Newton Clarke said that "the home is the child's first Bible, teaching through parental love and self-sacrifice the first lessons concerning God." We're living epistles, read by our children. What they read in large measure determines their goals and objectives in life. Make it your goal that God's love will so captivate your heart, your ambitions, and your desires that your children will fall in love with Him. Those who do are beautiful.

Chapter 12

EXPRESSING
YOUR BEAUTY

My favorite restaurant is Five Crowns in Corona del Mar, California. Eating there is sheer pleasure, a delightful blend of quality food and service, not to mention a beautiful, tranquil atmosphere. If eating is what you do at Five Crowns, sign me up, I'm a believer! I'll confess, repent, walk the aisle and maybe even shed a tear to become a "Five Crowner" for life. It's the total experience that makes a Five Crowns meal so beautiful.

How food is prepared and served makes all the difference in the world. Eight summers of assembly line camp food eaten in a crowded dining room with three hundred elbowing, screaming kids plus thirty wornout counselors would make an unbeliever out of anyone. If the abundant life is eating food at Chigger Creek Camp, then may I never live or have abundance! Sloppy food eaten with ravenous wolves spells disaster. Whatever it is, it isn't beautiful, or attractive. Beauty, however, is attractive. Whether it be princesses kissing frogs, ugly ducklings becoming swans or abused Cinderellas becoming belles of the ball, beauty is irresistible. Its presence is magnetic. It should come as no surprise, then, that God's strategy for evangelism is a beautiful bride.

A beautiful bride . . . that's the key to evangelism. Brides bypass intellects and capture hearts. Tough, calloused, hardened men are known to weep in their presence. Men of steel melt and their wives get misty eyed. Ideally, a bride is the epitome of all that's right and beautiful. She's a symbol of purity, hope, purpose, trust, love, beauty and wholeness in a world pockmarked with ugliness. Both Israel and the church are described as brides whose beauty is traced to God's love for them. Christ loves the church, His bride, in order that "He might present to Himself the church in all her glory, having no spot or wrinkle or any such thing; but that she should be holy and blameless" (Eph. 5:27,NASB).

Love in Evangelism

Unfortunately for many of us, evangelism is like trying to pick up a porcupine—we're not sure where to start. John 13:34-35 provides some good insights which help the process of evangelism to begin to happen. In this passage Jesus reminds His followers that the "world listens when Christians love." They will know we are followers of Christ if our lives are characterized by a genuine, observable love for one another. There are some important insights to be drawn from these verses.

First, caring relationships are unusual enough to capture the attention of the unbeliever. They will know we follow Christ if we *love* each other. We sometimes forget how unique it is to be part of a genuine, caring relationship. Many have no such experience, but secretly long for it.

Second, a caring, beautiful relationship *will* capture the attention of the searching heart. Our Lord said it would! "By this *all men will know* that you are My disciples, if you have love for one another" (John 13:35, NASB, italics added). We are living epistles whose lives are being read by all men. If the Holy Spirit writes the script, growing, healthy relationships are the fruit. When the world reads that kind of message, they recognize a divine author.

Third, caring relationships must be *available* to be observable. The salt must get out of the shaker, the light must not be hidden under a bushel. Evangelism is really a way of living—beautifully. It is displaying the universals of God's character: His love, His righteousness, His justice and faithfulness, through the particulars of everyday life. There is no impact without contact. Unfortunately, most believers have lost all significant contact with non-believers after knowing the Lord for two years.

Fourth, not all relationships between belivers are healthy, loving examples for the searching heart—"*if* you have love for one another." The church at Ephesus lost their love, and almost lost their candlestick (see Rev. 2:1-5). "Light" without love is not light.

The beautiful bride motif is especially intriguing because the bride is not a person, but rather *people in relationship.* Consequently, the beauty described is one of corporate function and relationship rather than outward form and appearance. God has designed the church as the primary context in which the possession of His nature surfaces and becomes an observable, tangible phenomenon. Not many are reading the revelation of God's grace revealed in Scripture. Many are reading the revelation of God revealed in your life and mine. Let's be certain the message is positive and magnetic!

The Greeks said an effective communicator possessed *ethos, pathos* and *logia.* These three qualities help us get a grasp on the way a "beautiful" living epistle should read. *Ethos* is the root from which we get our word "ethical." A person can be an excellent rhetorician and know the dynamics of persuasive speech, but if he is unethical, he's had it as far as effective communication is concerned. Paul told Timothy that leaders in the church must have impeccable credentials in the community and business world (see I Tim. 3:1-10). Paul also said we could speak with the eloquence of angels, but if love was missing, our eloquence comes through like the discordant crash of a cymbal (see I Cor. 13:1). To be ethical does not mean to be perfect. The ethical man owns up to failure when it occurs, makes wrongs right, and seeks forgiveness when he fails.

Our words "sympathy" and "empathy" are derived from the second quality, called *pathos*. The "words" of the gospel have added impact when "served" with a sense of genuine care and concern. Our friendships with non-Christians should be just that . . . friendships, not "friendships with a hook." When love is felt, the message is heard. When my wife, Ruthe, and I were on Campus Crusade staff at the University of Oregon we trained under Bud and Shirley Hinkson. I had the opportunity to tag along on several occasions when Bud shared the gospel with some collegians. Bud genuinely cared for people and it came through as he shared Christ. I am indebted to Bud for teaching me so much about *pathos*. We're not to be bounty hunters or scalp collectors. In sales terminology, we must reduce *relationship* tension before we introduce *task* tension. A caring, loving, sensitive person *becomes* good news before he ever verbalizes the good news.

Ethos and *pathos* tell me I must become good news before I verbalize it. Many have heard the "words" of the gospel, but not its "music." *Ethos* and *pathos* provide the "music" or beauty which creates an appetite for the words. Toynbee said that "most people have not rejected Christianity, but a caricature." Caricatures aren't beautiful!

Third, the effective communicator has *logia*, the

ability to "say the words" effectively. This is the area of strength in most evangelism training programs. They teach us the *content* of the gospel, how to "say the words." But they overlook the *context* in which the content can be most effectively shared.

A church elder was to have *ethos, pathos* and *logia.* He also was to be given to hospitality. His life and especially his home were to be an "open circle." This provided maximum exposure to the "music" of the gospel in a real life context. The "music" of the gospel is the evident outworking of God's grace in human experience. Its melody is heard as lives change, as bitterness disappears, as marriages become duets instead of duels.

Ethos, pathos and *logia* tell us that the effective evangelist needs to focus in two directions. First, he must cultivate significant, caring relationships and second, he must work towards developing a well-thought-out presentation of the *words* of the gospel.

If we are serious about evangelism, we must be serious about beauty. If we are serious about beauty, as we observed in a previous chapter, we must be serious about the beauty parlor (the church). Imagine the difficulty of being a salesman for a business with a poor corporate image in the community, or trying to communicate a message which promises hope, love, beauty and unity when your board of directors is known in the community for pessimism, divisiveness, pettiness and a lack of unity. If we are serious about evangelism, we must also be serious about our immediate home and family relationships. The godly home is probably God's most potent tool for exposing others to Christ. To do so it must be open for observation. The prospect of opening up our webs of relationships to the non-Christian creates fear in the hearts of many Christians. In a word, they don't know how to relate to the non-Christian in a significant manner.

Who Is Your Neighbor?

Christians often struggle to "evangelize" the person next to them on the plane or the "cold-turkey contact" on visitation night and yet overlook their most obvious mission field: their own neighborhood. We are commanded on numerous occasions to love our neighbors. Many Christians are "neighbors" to someone spatially and geographically, but most are neighbors to no one spiritually. We're masters at wrestling with the issue of "who is my neighbor?" as though evangelism was a problem of definition and selection. The goal is not to define who my neighbor is, but rather *to be* a neighbor. The word "neighbor" comes from a root meaning "to be near or close." To be a neighbor in the biblical sense is *to develop the ability and capacity to be near.* As stated earlier, there is no impact without contact. Yet "nearness" presupposes distance. The true neighbor is the person who has overcome the barriers to nearness. There are many such barriers which keep people at a distance. The fear of rejection is a big one. After all, aren't Christians "peculiar people," and who wants to get close to a peculiar anything?

Another barrier is the fear of judgment by other Christians. Anyone trying to evangelize outside of the stained glass aquarium on Sunday morning runs this risk. Many never become neighbors because they have become prisoners of other people's expectations. Some fear compromise, others suffer from unbelief. For many it's a matter of priorities. Christ's great commission hasn't made the "top ten" on their list.

Paul became near (and dear) to a motley crew in the port town of Corinth. Believe me, there were plenty of obstacles to nearness in this seafarers' watering hole. The secret of Paul's success is given in I Cor. 9:22. "I have become all things to all men, that I may by all means save some" (NASB). In this remarkable verse Paul illustrates three significant factors in becoming near.

First, we become a neighbor when we are willing to become *all things* to all men. Here we see the principle of *cultural flexibility*. Paul was sensitive to the background of the people he dealt with. In verses 20-22 he says, "To the Jews I became as a Jew, that I might win Jews; . . . to those who are without law, as without law . . . that I might win those who are without law. To the weak I became weak, that I might win the weak . . ." (NASB).

The greatest barriers to effective evangelism are cultural, not theological. One night I drove past a little fly-by-night circus outfit getting set up for a two or three night stand. I would have some monumental cultural barriers, and probably some prejudices, to overcome in attempting to reach them for Christ. Somewhere in my past I picked up the idea that circuses are not healthy places for Christians to be, and those associated with the circus are less than wholesome people. I'm sure such information is not entirely accurate, yet it colors my feelings towards those involved in this lifestyle. Setting such feeling aside, there would still be some difficult hurdles to overcome. They have a language all of their own. They have a philosophy of life and a value system which I would have to understand and adjust to. I'm certain that if I began to be a "neighbor" to these people I would discover they can be loving, caring, God-fearing like anyone else. To really minister effectively to them, it would be important to become naturalized citizens of their world, and see life from their perspective.

This principle of cultural accommodation means that I am not to blast my way through the customs and conscience of other people. If I am becoming near to a Jew, I must respect his culture and heritage. In some settings I must limit my liberty so as to not offend. In every situation the effective neighbor makes every effort not to willingly insult the beliefs, customs, and prejudices of others. To be "all things" is not to relax standards, but to develop flexi-

139

bility when it comes to matters without moral significance. It means making myself flexible to another man's interests, concerns, conscience, circumstances, opinions and background. I don't expect my "neighbors" to meet my standards before I develop significant relationships with them.

Paul's becoming "all things" worked out of a particular mindset which is crucial to the process. In verse 19 he says, "For though I am free from all men, I have made myself a slave to all, that I might win the more" (NASB). Paul voluntarily set aside his rights so that he could assume the posture of beauty, the posture of a slave. Genuine self-denial in behalf of others is a powerful tool for the gospel. When an ethical person demonstrates a genuine, sacrificial concern for others, people are inclined to pay attention.

The key to fruitfulness is death. John 12:24 says "Verily, verily, I say unto you, Except a corn of wheat fall into the ground and die, it abideth alone: but if it die, it bringeth forth much fruit" (KJV). The one certain way of expanding the usefulness of my life is to bury it. God means for us to have practical moments of bowing before Him and letting Him pat the soil over our heads. There must be regular points in my life when I deliberately die to the logical thing to do. At times I must die to ease and quietness, die to the exercise of power and rights and live as a servant for others. We will reap what we sow, and more than we sow.

Second, we become a neighbor when we are willing to become all things to *all men*. God is no respecter of persons, and we shouldn't be either. The unlovely and unlikely should be within the focus of our vision. Life is full of lonely travelers like the man on his way to Jericho. Thieves saw him as a victim to exploit and left him badly wounded. The priest and Levite came upon the wounded traveler and kept going. They saw him as an inconvenience to avoid. The innkeeper saw him as a customer to serve. The Lord singled out the good Samaritan as the one who knew what it was to love his neighbor. The Samaritan saw the lonely traveler (a complete stranger) as someone to love regardless of the cost and inconvenience (see Luke 10:30-37). The neighbor becomes all things to all men, especially those who are badly wounded by life.

In a youth-oriented culture there is a lot of truth in the bumper sticker which reminds us that "Dirty old men need love too." If I were traveling to Jericho and came upon the T.V. character, Maude, lying mortally wounded in the ditch, my first inclination would be to bury her. To me she is the epitome of corrupted womanhood, even though I often laugh so hard I weep while watching the program. If she were a real person living next door, I'd have the challenge of a lifetime being a neighbor to her. For God to use me as an instrument to bring such a one to Christ, I would have to accept her, overlook her personal viewpoints, take an interest in her interests, and demonstrate a loving, serving spirit. I believe in miracles!

By All Means

Third, Paul says we become neighbors by being all things to all men, so that *by all possible means* we might save some. The means are limited only by our own creativity. A "means" is whatever is necessary to bring me into significant contact with my unsaved neighbor in such a way that he hears the music of the gospel. It may happen on a tennis court, on a boat, on the golf course, at a meal together, at a football game, over the back fence or through working on a project together. It could happen at an evangelistic dinner, a home Bible study and even in the "stained glass aquarium." Find out what interests him and take an interest. Find out his needs and be part of their solution. Give, serve, love, care, listen and the beauty of it all will make its power felt.

141

People respond to beauty, especially when it's available for them to see and share. When the beauty that begins in the heart shapes the home and flows out to touch the lives of those searching for it, the message is heard. Try becoming *all things* to *all men*, so that by *all possible means* you might win some.

God is beauty. As partakers of His nature we can be beautiful. As objects of His craftsmanship, we are becoming beautiful. Forget the paint and pillows. Express what you possess and look out. Beauty is irresistable!

The Ultimate Lifestyle by Tim Timmons

Experiencing a *supernatural* relationship with God, and displaying the effects of that experience everyday— that's the ultimate lifestyle!

- Who lives it?
- Where is it lived?
- How is it lived?

Tim Timmons answers these simple but profound questions, as he tells the story of his own dawning to an awareness of God in daily life and the joy he finds in sharing God's reality with the world he encounters.

He brings the question of knowing God's will for your life into Biblical focus, leading the reader to an appreciation of the full, unique Christian lifestyle— the lifestyle that not only stands *up* to reality, but stands *out* in our world!

Paper $3.98 DTIM01